BECOME WHAT YOU BELIEVE

LUTHER MCKINSTRY III

CHARISMA
HOUSE

Luther McKinstry has done us all a favor by masterfully and simply giving us the tools to move forward. Life is a journey. I think reading this book will point you in the right direction.

—BISHOP MICHAEL PITTS
CORNERSTONE CHURCH

Become What You Believe is more than a book; it's a blueprint for transformation. Bishop Luther McKinstry doesn't just teach faith; he shows readers how to live it until belief becomes being. Every page ignites conviction, clarity, and courage to step into the life God intended.

—DR. DHARIUS DANIELS
LEAD PASTOR, CHANGE CHURCH
AUTHOR, *RELATIONAL INTELLIGENCE*

My dear friend Bishop Luther McKinstry III writes with a pastor's heart and a believer's conviction. *Become What You Believe* is a passionate invitation to trust God's promises, to pray with confidence, and to live in alignment with divine purpose. I deeply appreciate Bishop McKinstry's desire to call God's people into deeper faith and wholehearted obedience. His words remind us that belief is not passive; it is active, formative, and transformative. Those who read this work with an open heart will find encouragement to live out their faith with renewed courage and clarity.

—BISHOP MARK J. CHIRONNA, PhD, CHURCH ON THE LIVING EDGE
MARK CHIRONNA MINISTRIES, LONGWOOD, FLORIDA

Become What You Believe is more than a book—it is a prophetic call to action. Bishop Luther McKinstry III has masterfully penned a spiritual roadmap that challenges believers not only to declare their faith but to *embody* it. With clarity, conviction, and biblical precision, he leads the reader into a deeper dimension of prayer, identity, and purpose.

This work ignites faith, fortifies the soul, and equips the believer to live fully in alignment with heaven's agenda. It is both practical and deeply spiritual—a book that will not just inspire you but *transform* the way you walk with God.

For every believer ready to move from belief to manifestation, from promise to power, this is your guide.

—BISHOP GEORGE G. BLOOMER
BESTSELLING AUTHOR OF *WITCHCRAFT IN THE PEWS*

I could not be prouder of Bishop Luther McKinstry and the powerful message found within these pages. From the very first story, his words capture the heart of faith, courage, and the transformative power of prayer. This book is not just a testimony of his journey—it's an invitation for every reader to dive deeper into God's presence and discover the strength that only prayer can bring. As his mother and fellow servant of the gospel, I see in his writing the same passion and perseverance that have always defined his ministry. This is a work that will inspire, uplift, and renew the faith of all who read it.

—BISHOP PAT MCKINSTRY
SENIOR PASTOR, WORSHIP CENTER OF TOLEDO

The idea of evolving is deceptive because it depends on natures shifts and can mislead your life's course into an anti-Christ embrace of the culture. However, to Be-Come is your sure path toward coming into being who God says you are, bypassing natures fickle ebbs and flows. This book will bring you closer to Be-Coming who God designed for your life!

—BISHOP B DWAYNE HARDIN
LEAD PASTOR, THE EMBASSY ATL CHURCH
PRESIDENT, THE MILLENNIUM MASTERS, INC. FELLOWSHIP

As I read *Become What You Believe*, my heart was stirred with renewed expectation for my NEXT! Bishop McKinstry doesn't simply write about faith; he imparts it. This book carries a prophetic urgency, calling believers to rise from passivity into divine identity, from prayer as routine into prayer as a world changing force. These pages are not just to be read but to be lived. If you are ready to step into the future God has already declared about you, this book will be your launching pad.

—DR. TL PENNY
SENIOR PASTOR, SHABACH WORLD CATHEDRAL
AUTHOR, LIFE COACH

Bishop/Prophet Luther McKinstry has written more than a book—he has released a prophetic mandate in print. *Become What You Believe* is not just fresh content; it's a catalyst for transformation. The book's unique angle makes it a must read. Truly, this is a book that can change lives.

The insight contained here is both fresh and timeless—rooted deeply in Scripture, the very foundation of our faith, yet spoken with the urgency of the Spirit for this generation. Bishop McKinstry is stirring the body of Christ to see that belief is not passive; it is creative. Every page breathes conviction and hope, urging the believer to align their thoughts with truth until life mirrors their faith.

This work is more than a book—it's a mirror and a movement. It challenges what you've settled for, brings to light what's been hidden, and confirms what heaven has already spoken over you. *Become What You Believe* is not just a good read—it's a prophetic experience that has the potential to reshape your thinking, living, and leading. Those who read with open hearts will be inspired to change their lives.

—BISHOP LISTON PAGE II, DMIN., STM, M.DIV.

Just as the ascending Psalms accompanied pilgrims as they journeyed to Jerusalem for feast days, this collection of prayers by Bishop McKinstry looks to accompany those of us who believe in and experience the Kingdom of God as the "Here but Not Yet."

Certainly, this is a work to include in developing a contemplative rule of life.

—THE MOST REV. EMILIO ALVAREZ, PHD
PRESIDING BISHOP UNION, CHARISMATICALLY ORTHODOX CHURCHES
VICE PRESIDENT AND DEAN OF ACADEMIC AFFAIRS, COLGATE ROCHESTER
CROZER DIVINITY SCHOOL

Bishop Chad MacDonald's new book, *Become What You Believe*, could not be more timely for the generation we live in today. In an era when culture is pushing the church toward an identity crisis, Bishop McKinstry calls us back to the foundations of faith—not just to profess what we believe but to live it with conviction, power, and authenticity.

At the core of his message is a simple yet profound truth: You will never become what you refuse to believe. This book reminds us that belief is more than mental assent—it is alignment with the heart of God. Bishop McKinstry teaches that our transformation begins by being anchored in relationship with the Father. From that intimacy flows boldness, confidence, and spiritual authority. It is this closeness to God that challenges us to examine ourselves, heal from within, and walk in the fullness of who God has called us to be. If you're ready to move from believing about God to becoming everything He has called you to be, this book is your next step.

—BISHOP SCOTT KING
JUDAH CHURCH

This is not just another devotional; it's a Spirit-led guide to living out the truth of God's Word every single day. Page by page, Bishop McKinstry challenges you to speak what you believe, pray what you expect, and become all that God has declared you to be.

If you've ever felt stuck, weary, or unsure of your purpose, this book will remind you that your faith has power—creative, life-shaping power. *Become What You Believe* will equip you to align your heart, words, and actions with heaven's agenda so you can step boldly into your God-given destiny.

—JONATHAN MILLER
SENIOR PASTOR, NEW BEGINNINGS CHURCH

Become What You Believe is a compelling reminder that faith was never meant to remain abstract. It was designed to take form in the life of the believer. This book carries a clear and convicting message: transformation begins when belief becomes behavior and conviction translates into consistent action. This work will reignite faith, renew focus, and restore courage to all who dare to believe again.

—BISHOP MIAH WHITE
LEAD PASTOR, THE WORSHIP CENTER

Life will test what you say you believe. You can shout "favor!" on Sunday, but it's those Monday mornings, when the bills, the heartbreak, or the silence hits, when your faith gets its real workout. That's why this book hit me right in the spirit. Bishop McKinstry isn't just talking about faith—he's teaching us how to walk it out: step by step, word by word, prayer by prayer. *Become What You Believe* is like a spiritual mirror reminding you that you're not waiting on God—He's waiting on you to believe who He already said you are.

—LISA RAYE MCCOY
ACTRESS/SAG-AFTRA

The message of this book is so timely. Bishop Luther McKinstry will lead you from the furnace of life—where your relationship with God is refined— to the mountain of His presence, where heaven's agenda is activated in the believer's daily life.

Become What You Believe is a breath of fresh air for discouraged and disheartened people, believers and non-believers alike, who feel trapped in mundane and mediocre existence. A road map to personal transformation, this book is a must-read for those who will consider the wisdom of biblical principles not just to believe but to become!

—BISHOP MILLICENT HUNTER, EdD, DMin
PRESIDING PRELATE, WORSHIP CENTER WORLDWIDE FELLOWSHIP OF
CHURCHES

Two biblical Hebraic terms fittingly describe Bishop Luther McKinstry's calling: *navi* (prophet) and *malakh* (messenger). He carries a word that confronts, clarifies, and summons. I have known him and his parents for more than twenty-five years, from his early pursuit of scriptural wisdom to the seasoned maturity evident in his ministry today. What he has received, he now gives: instruction grounded in Scripture and conveyed with conviction.

This book conveys that wisdom, directing the mind and heart toward matters of lasting consequence—the will and purpose of God.

—ED NELSON
RETIRED EXECUTIVE, ASSEMBLIES OF GOD NETWORK

The transformative journey outlined in this book will unlock the potential within you and enable you to become who you are meant to be. *Become What You Believe* is not just a reflection on faith; it's a call to action, inspiring us to trust in God's plan and actively pursue the life He designed for us. If you're seeking encouragement on your spiritual journey, this book is a must-read.

—BISHOP TODD M. HALL, DSL
PRESIDING PRELATE, SHABACH CHRISTIAN CHURCH FELLOWSHIP

Whether you are a seasoned leader, a new believer, or someone seeking to reignite your faith, *Become What You Believe* challenges and empowers you to become everything God has destined you to be.

Every pastor, intercessor, servant-leader, and believer who desires to walk in the fullness of their divine purpose will find in this book a road map to spiritual maturity and victorious living. Bishop McKinstry's writing is both prophetic and pastoral, profound yet practical—a guide for all who are ready to move from inspiration to transformation.

—JULIA WHITEHURST WADE
APOSTOLIC COUNCIL LEADER, JOINT COLLEGE OF AFRICAN AMERICAN
PENTECOSTAL BISHOPS

As a proud son of Fremont, Bishop Luther McKinstry III continues to inspire far beyond our city's borders. *Become What You Believe* is a powerful reminder that faith, perseverance, and purpose can transform not only individuals but entire communities. His words reflect the heart of Fremont—resilience, hope, and belief in what is possible. I commend Bishop McKinstry for sharing a message that uplifts and challenges us all to live out our faith boldly.

—DANNY SANCHEZ
MAYOR, FREMONT, OHIO

While the author has made every effort to provide accurate, up-to-date source information at the time of publication, statistics and other data are constantly updated. Neither the publisher nor the author assumes any responsibility for errors or for changes that occur after publication. Further, the publisher and author do not have any control over and do not assume any responsibility for third-party websites or their content.

For more resources like this, visit MyCharismaShop.com.

Cataloging-in-Publication Data is on file with the Library of Congress.
International Standard Book Number: 978-1-63641-559-8
E-book ISBN: 978-1-63641-560-4

1 2025
Printed in the United States of America

Most Charisma Media products are available at special quantity discounts for bulk purchase for sales promotions, premiums, fund-raising, and educational needs. For details, call us at (407) 333-0600 or visit our website at charismamedia.com.

DEDICATION

&

This book is dedicated to three mothers in Zion—women whose prayers covered me, whose faith carried me, and whose love refused to let me go—even when I was not walking worthy of God's grace and mercy.

To Mother Clara Moore, Mother Ruby Slack, and Mother Hazel Page—your intercession shaped my destiny. You stood in the gap when I could not stand for myself. You spoke my name before the throne when I had lost my way.

Though you are no longer present in the physical realm, your spiritual fingerprints are on every page of my life. I am the fruit of your labor, the evidence of your prayers, and the living testimony of your faithfulness.

I only wish you could see the harvest your prayers produced.

CONTENTS

FOREWORD

IN EVERY GENERATION God raises voices that call His people back to the simplicity and power of believing Him at His Word. *Become What You Believe* by Luther McKinstry III is one such call—a timely and transformative guide for anyone longing to deepen their prayer life and see tangible results through faith-filled declarations.

Rooted in the powerful words of Jesus from Matthew 9:29 (MSG), "Become what you believe," this book reminds us that the life we live is directly connected to the faith we hold. In a world filled with uncertainty, fear, and spiritual distraction, this work realigns our focus on what truly matters: the unchanging promises of God and the invitation to partner with Him through prayer.

This is not merely a collection of prayers; it is a road map for personal transformation. Each chapter draws from the rich well of Scripture, offering readers topical prayers that cover every area of life—from peace to prosperity, from healing to revival, from family to victory. What sets this book apart is its intentional design to help readers not only pray but believe and become what God has spoken over them.

Luther McKinstry III has skillfully combined biblical truth with practical application, weaving together timeless principles such as Adoration, Confession, Thanksgiving, and Supplication (ACTS) with declarations that speak directly to the heart and spirit. This book equips you to not just speak words but to speak living words—words that align with heaven's agenda and invite heaven's power into your daily life.

As you journey through these pages, you will be challenged to:

+ Believe God for more, even in impossible situations.

+ Speak life and destiny over yourself and your loved ones.

+ Walk in spiritual authority and victory.

+ Expect God's abundance, provision, and peace—right in the middle of the storm.

Whether you are new to prayer or a seasoned intercessor, *Become What You Believe* will stir your faith, ignite your hope, and anchor your heart in the unwavering truth of God's Word. I encourage you not only to read this book but to use it, declare it, and live it—so that you, too, will become what you believe.

—JOHN ECKHARDT
OVERSEER, CRUSADERS MINISTRIES
BEST-SELLING AUTHOR OF *PRAYERS THAT ROUT DEMONS*

ACKNOWLEDGMENTS

FIRST AND FOREMOST, I want to give honor and gratitude to my parents, Overseer Luther and Bishop Pat McKinstry. Thank you for bringing me up in a godly home where faith was not just taught but lived. Thank you for showing me what it means to love God, serve people, and walk with integrity.

The foundation you laid—through your prayers, your guidance, your example, and your unwavering belief in me—is the reason I stand today. Every chapter of my life and every word of this book were built upon the sacrifices you made and the principles you instilled.

I am who I am because of the home you created and the legacy you modeled. I pray that this work honors that legacy and reflects the seeds of faith you planted in me from the very beginning.

PREFACE

I WAS NEVER SUPPOSED to end up in prison—not once, and certainly not twice. I came from a good home, with a praying mother and a loving father. I grew up in church, saw God move, and knew His call was on my life. But knowing the truth isn't the same as living it. And I wasn't.

Little by little, I started chasing the wrong things. At first, it was curiosity, then compromise, and eventually outright rebellion. What I thought would make me stronger only revealed how weak I truly was. What I thought would set me free only chained me tighter. I longed to be somebody—to be seen, respected, and admired. And for a while, it looked like I had it all. I was an athlete, a soldier, a ladies' man, and eventually, a rising name on the streets.

But when I looked in the mirror, I didn't recognize the man staring back. Outwardly, I had money in my pocket, women on my arm, and influence in the wrong places. Inwardly, I was hollow. I was dying a slow death. Twice, I found myself behind bars, stripped of the image I worked so hard to build. More than once, I stood face-to-face with the reality that I could lose everything—my freedom, my future, and even my life.

I'll never forget the day when undercover agents slammed me to the ground in a drug bust. I told the man who set me up, "I'm looking at a dead man." What I didn't realize was that the dead man was me. Scripture says, "The wages of sin is death," and I was cashing every check (Rom. 6:23).

Yet grace has a way of chasing you down. Even when I was far from God, my mother's prayers and my father's love were like a hedge around me. I should have been dead. I should have been forgotten. But the Lord wouldn't let go.

The day I finally surrendered, everything changed. Jesus didn't just forgive me—He transformed me. He didn't merely deliver me from the mess I created; He began to teach me how to walk in His promises, how to align my words and my life with His truth, and how to become what I believed.

That's what this book is about. If God can take a broken, addicted, angry, prideful man like me and turn me into a preacher of His Word, then there's no limit to what He can do in your life. This isn't a book about what He brought me out of; it is an invitation to step into what

He is calling all of us to: the reality of what Jesus purchased for us on the cross—peace, health, victory, and much more.

> **Even when I was far from God, my mother's prayers and my father's love were like a hedge around me. I should have been dead. I should have been forgotten. But the Lord wouldn't let go.**

So many Christians live bound and depressed, no different from those who don't know Jesus. They don't live as sons and daughters of God. They live broke, busted, and disgusted, instead of walking in the power of God, experiencing unspeakable joy, and having provision in every season.

That used to be me. But my parents never lost sight of who God had called me to be. They prayed that I would serve Him wholeheartedly, use my gifts for His glory, and walk in the blessings that come with obedience. And God answered those prayers! Today, I minister because my parents dared to take God at His Word and believe that prayer could change things.

WHAT DO YOU BELIEVE?

When the Lord gave me the title of this book, He led me to a familiar passage in the Gospel of Matthew: a story about two blind men.

> As Jesus left the house, he was followed by two blind men crying out, "Mercy, Son of David! Mercy on us!" When Jesus got home, the blind men went in with him. Jesus said to them, "Do you really believe I can do this?" They said, "Why, yes, Master!" He touched their eyes and said, *"Become what you believe."* It happened. They saw. Then Jesus became very stern. "Don't let a soul know how this happened." But they were hardly out the door before they started blabbing it to everyone they met.
> —MATTHEW 9:27–31, MSG, EMPHASIS ADDED

Now, how could two blind men follow someone they could not see? These men must have known Jesus stood nearby because they asked Him to have mercy on them. But at the end of the day, they had to rely on faith that they were in the presence of God. They had to believe that they were in the right place at the right time for their healing.

These men had heard about Jesus, but they didn't just know who He was. When Jesus asked the men whether they believed He could heal them, they said, "Yes, Master." And as He touched their eyes, He made the statement that resonated with me and motivated me to write this book: "Become what you believe." Instantly, the two men were able to see. These men *believed* the word Jesus spoke over them. They believed He was able to heal them! They believed their blindness would be a thing of the past. There is so much you and I can get out of this word. The following are a few highlights I want to impress on you.

As Romans 10:17 teaches, faith comes by hearing and hearing by the Word of God. As it was for the blind men, so it is for us. We *must believe* the Word of God. We must know God's thoughts toward us, which are found in His Word. His Word teaches us that His plans are for us to prosper, be successful, and have a great future.

What would you become if the Lord were to tell you today, "Become what you believe"? Before you can become healed of that sickness or disease, you have to believe Jesus is the Healer. Before You can become wealthy or financially sufficient, you have to believe the Lord is the Provider. Before you can see your family restored and set free of generational curses, you have to believe God is the Deliverer. In the kingdom seeing isn't believing— *believing is seeing*. If you want to see God do what He promised in His Word, then you have to become a person who believes without doubt, fear, or hesitation that God will do what He said.

The words *become* and *believe* have something in common: the two-letter word *be*. We must *be* who God calls us to *be*. If two blind men knew enough to follow Jesus, catch what He declared, and believe their eyesight would be restored, how much more do you and I need to take God at His Word? We must change our way of thinking and start believing everything God declared so we can become what we're supposed to be and access all we're supposed to have. Jesus is speaking the same word to us that He spoke to those blind men more than two thousand years ago: "Become what you believe."

> **In the kingdom seeing isn't believing—*believing is seeing*.**

We need to become what we believe, and that happens as we pray God's Word—because we know that God's Word is His will. I've done my best to make this book as user-friendly as possible. Each chapter focuses on a unique topic and includes key verses that reveal what the Word says about that issue. I also framed those scriptures into prayers, so you can use them to speak God's Word over your life.

This book is meant to be a resource. Jump right to the chapter you need. Use it in your personal prayer time, at corporate prayer meetings, or in Bible studies. God's Word is living and active; it is sharper than a two-edged sword, and it will accomplish that for which it is sent (Heb. 4:12; Isa. 55:11). So don't just read the Word, believe it. If you take God at His Word and pray the Scriptures back to Him, your life will be changed. I'm living proof.

So are you ready to become what you believe? Let's begin!

TAKE HOLD OF THE POWER OF PRAYER

A S A YOUNG boy, I often found myself in the most peculiar situations—times when my curiosity collided with reckless courage. One moment stands out in my memory as both humbling and transformative. On that day, brimming with youthful energy and a craving to be seen and accepted, I chased after a group of older boys at the community pool. Confident in themselves, they began running and diving into the deep end with ease. Not wanting to be left out and determined to prove I was just as brave, I decided to jump in too.

There was just one problem: I had never learned to swim! I didn't have a single lesson or even an afternoon of paddling in the shallow end. But in that moment I wasn't thinking about my inexperience. I saw what others were doing and assumed I could do it too. My desire to fit in overtook my better judgment. I sprinted toward the pool's edge, closed my eyes, and jumped in.

You can imagine what happened next: chaos, panic, flailing limbs. In less than a minute, lifeguards and onlookers sprang into action. I scrambled about, trying to make it to the surface, but the truth is, I was drowning. By God's grace someone rescued me. My mother tells me I was left momentarily breathless, and a lifeguard had to perform CPR. After seconds that seemed like an eternity to my parents, I regained my breath and collapsed into their arms.

Recognizing both my fear and my potential, my parents enrolled me in swimming lessons that very week. I spent the next year learning the basics—floating, paddling, breathing underwater—skills that would eventually give me confidence in the water.

The following summer I found myself back at the same pool. This time my father stood on the edge with me. He knew I was nervous as I remembered the trauma of the year before. But he gently encouraged me, saying, "I'll be right here. Just jump. I won't let you fall." His voice—steady, sure, and full of love—cut through my fear. So I jumped. And this time someone was there to catch me.

My friends, prayer is just like this. When we first begin to pray, we are often like an inexperienced child, jumping into something deep and mysterious without fully knowing what we're doing. We may hear others praying eloquently and walking confidently in their faith and think we can and should do the same. So we dive in—arms flailing, words unsure—hoping that somehow we'll touch God's heart.

But then comes the confusion, the frustration: "Why am I still struggling?" "Why doesn't it feel like God is hearing me?" "Why do my prayers seem unanswered?" We begin to feel like we're drowning in our own uncertainty, and many give up at this stage. But, beloved, just as I was enrolled in swimming lessons to teach me how to survive and eventually thrive in the water, God wants to bring us into a season during which we learn how to pray effectively, develop spiritual endurance, and grow in discernment. It is through intentional time in God's presence and Word that we build the strength to swim in the depths of prayer without fear. And it is by praying His Word in faith that we become everything it says we can be.

PRAYING THE SCRIPTURES

Prayer is not a religious ritual. It's not a box to check off during our morning routine. It is a divine connection point between heaven and earth. It is a lifeline to the Creator—the language of intimacy between a Father and His child. Through prayer we don't simply submit our "wish list" to God; we align ourselves with His will and His Word. Prayer is how we participate in the unfolding of God's purposes on earth.

James 5:16 reminds us, "The effective, fervent prayer of a righteous man avails much." This kind of heartfelt prayer doesn't develop overnight. It is cultivated through discipline, obedience, and spiritual maturity. Just as I had to learn how to breathe, kick, and stroke in the pool, we must learn to listen to the Spirit of God and declare His Word in prayer.

To dive deeper into this truth, consider this powerful verse from Psalm 103:20: "Bless the LORD, you His angels, who excel in strength, who do His word, heeding the voice of His word." The implications of this verse are remarkable. The voice of God's Word activates the angels of heaven. That means when believers pray His Word, they dispatch angelic forces. When we pray according to Scripture, we are not just whispering hopeful thoughts into the sky; we are sending forth declarations that move heaven into action.

This is why praying the Scriptures is so important. When we take God's promises, prophecies, and principles and return them to Him in prayer, we are essentially placing His Word back into His mouth. Isaiah 55:11 affirms this, saying, "So shall My word be that goes forth from My mouth; it shall not return to Me void, but it shall accomplish what I please, and it shall prosper in the thing for which I sent it."

> **Prayer can't be something we do in reaction to problems; we have to see it as a force that can shape our lives and destinies.**

When we pray God's Word, we align our will with His, causing His power to manifest in our situations. Prayer becomes more than a religious discipline; it becomes strategic warfare, infused with heavenly authority.

But again, to get to this level of power in prayer, we must first go through a season of learning, just as I did with swimming. We must study the Scriptures and build our faith muscles. We must tune our ears to the voice of the Holy Spirit—our instructor—who beckons us: "Jump. I'm right here. I won't let you fall."

Prayer can't be something we do in reaction to problems; we have to see it as a force that can shape our lives and destinies. Through prayer we declare healing, unlock provision, bind the enemy's plans, and loose blessings from heaven. It is through prayer that we receive peace, clarity, and strength. And it is through prayer that we draw closer to the heart of God and learn to trust Him more every day.

My friends, whether you're still flailing in the shallow end or confidently swimming in the depths, know this: Prayer will transform your life. So keep listening for His voice. Keep praying His Word. And never forget this: Someone is on the other side, ready to catch you.

DON'T LET YOUR MIRACLE STAY TRAPPED IN YOUR MIND

The mind is more than a place of thoughts and memories; it is a divine instrument that holds the capacity to shape our reality, especially when activated through the power of speech. Scientific research has established a direct connection between the brain and the mouth. The composition of

bacteria in the mouth is associated with mental health symptoms; adults
with missing teeth are more likely to develop cognitive impairment and
dementia. Infections and diseases in the mouth can be sources of mind-
altering conditions.[1]

This is not just science; this is Scripture. Proverbs 18:21 says, "Death
and life are in the power of the tongue." Jesus said in Mark 11:23 that
"whoever says to this mountain, 'Be removed and be cast into the sea,' and
does not doubt in his heart, but believes that those things he says will be
done, he will have whatever he says." The bottom line is, your miracle can
be trapped between your mind and your mouth.

The Hebrew word *yāḏ* means "hand," and it is a symbol of power, direction, and ability.[2] Just as your hand reaches to take hold of things in the
natural, words spoken from your mind reach into the spirit realm and
cause them to become reality. It's not enough for you to desire something
or to just think about it; you must release that desire with your mouth.
That is how your faith is activated. Again, death and life are in the power
of the tongue. Your voice is the spiritual hand that grabs hold of your
answered prayer.

> **Your miracle can be trapped between
> your mind and your mouth.**

We must stop treating our thoughts as passive and our prayers as routine. The mind is a gateway. When you speak what God has shown you
and what His Word declares, you shift the atmosphere, causing it to align
with what heaven has declared over your life. This is not an empty affir-
mation; this is the biblical law of confession.

Don't let your miracle stay trapped in your mind. Open your mouth,
speak in faith, and release what God has placed inside you. When working
together, the mind and mouth carry the power to birth the supernatural.
This coupled with faith leads to transformation.

THREE DIMENSIONS OF FAITH

Without faith it is impossible to please God (Heb. 11:6)—which means
that without faith it is impossible to be effective in prayer. When we pray
the Word of God, we must couple that with our faith to see the results of
heaven.

Hebrews 11:1 declares, "Now faith is the substance of things hoped for, the evidence of things not seen." This verse is a powerful cornerstone of Christian belief, offering not just a definition of faith but a glimpse into how it operates in real time. I want to quickly unpack the three dimensions of faith revealed in this scripture: "now faith," "through faith," and "by faith." I relate them to something many of us understand: navigating traffic.

Now faith

"Now faith" is not yesterday's belief or tomorrow's hope; it's urgent and activated in the present moment. Now faith doesn't hesitate. It's the kind of faith that makes a declaration before you see the solution. It's like when you're in gridlocked traffic, and your GPS reroutes you. You *immediately* trust and respond to that new direction, even if you don't fully see where it's taking you.

Through faith

"Through faith" is how we travel the long road. It's not instant; it's the process. Hebrews 11 is full of testimonies of saints who endured trials, dangers, and uncertainties *through faith*. I think of it like driving down the interstate and seeing bumper-to-bumper traffic. You're still moving, but the journey is slower, and every exit tempts you to quit. But through faith causes you to endure. Through faith you keep your hands on the wheel and your eyes on the promise. You believe that even if it's taking longer than expected, you are still going to reach your destination.

By faith

"By faith" is directional. It's when you shift and move differently than what makes sense in the natural. Sometimes you're on the main highway of life, but God tells you to take the bypass, a route meant to take you *around* congestion, construction, or delay. That's what "by faith" does. It reroutes you around things that could have slowed or stopped your progress.

You may not even understand why you're taking that unfamiliar road. But by faith you trust that God's navigation system sees what you can't. He's taking you around betrayal, heartbreak, and delay so you arrive at your destination in His timing, not man's.

When we talk about faith, we're not just talking about a spiritual concept; we're talking about a movement system. Now faith says, "Go"; through faith says, "Endure"; and by faith says, "Adjust." You need all three. There are times you must act immediately (now), times you must hold steady (through), and times you must change direction entirely (by).

Faith is how we move forward when nothing around us says we can. It's trusting God's GPS, knowing He sees the road ahead, even when all we can see is a traffic jam.

This is why we pray. Prayer activates our faith so that we believe God will be faithful to perform His Word.

GOD WILL KEEP HIS WORD

God makes us an incredible promise in 2 Corinthians 1:20: "For all the promises of God in Him are Yes, and in Him Amen, to the glory of God through us."

We are *not* praying to a God who makes empty promises. In fact, He will never back down on His Word, because if He goes against His Word, He goes against Himself. But whatever God said is supported by heaven.

This is why we should be excited to pray. God *will* keep His Word, and as our trust in Him matures, we come to see that His timing is perfect. Just because we don't receive the answer right away doesn't mean He has denied us. There are simply opportune times that await the moments of release. We must trust that God is working behind the scenes and what He says about our lives, our families, and our futures will come to pass.

GOD'S PROMISES = SPIRITUAL ACCESS

Have you ever promised a child something without giving it to them immediately? They'll keep asking for it until you finally respond with a "Not right now." Then the child will say, "But you promised." Most of us will look that child right in the eyes and say, "I will do it. I promise." This gives them the assurance that we will do what we said. They have access to what is not in front of them because they trust the one who made the promise.

This is exactly what the promises of God do for us. The Father's promises give us access to what is to come, even though we must wait expectantly for the fulfillment. This is why we pray what God has said! Knowing that my words match heaven's promises gives me confidence that I will receive what God has lined up for me in the spirit. This is why we can say we have peace in the middle of disruption and why we can say we are victorious when most would say they are defeated. We are secure in the promises of God, and because God said it, we know it can't be diminished and won't be stopped. A delay is not a denial!

FOUR COMPONENTS OF PRAYER

As we remind God of His Word in prayer, four components should be present in our prayers: adoration, confession, thanksgiving, and supplication.

1. *Adoration* is when we lift our hearts in worship, focusing on who God is—His majesty, power, and glory—rather than what He gives.

2. *Confession* is when we humbly acknowledge our sins and shortcomings before Him, seeking His mercy and forgiveness through Christ.

3. *Thanksgiving* is expressing gratitude for God's goodness, blessings, and faithfulness in our lives.

4. *Supplication* is bringing our requests and petitions before the Lord, asking for His help, provision, and intervention for ourselves and others.

To make it practical, the following is a sample prayer that includes all four components.

Adoration

Father, we bless and honor You for Your power, glory, victory, and majesty. Lord, all that is in heaven and in earth is Yours. Yours is the kingdom. You are exalted over everything! Riches and honor come from You. You reign over all. In Your hand is greatness. You give strength to all. (See 1 Chronicles 29:11–14.)

Confession

Jesus, 1 John 1:9 says that if we confess our sins to You, You are faithful to forgive and purify us from all unrighteousness. I repent for those times when I've missed the mark, and I thank You for forgiving me. Cleanse me of my sins and make me new, in Jesus' name.

Thanksgiving

> *Thank You, Lord, for forgiving and redeeming me. Father, I bless You for Your great love and for all the wonderful things You have done for me. I give You my thanks as a sacrifice. I will sing of Your glorious acts toward me* (Ps. 107:21–22).

Supplication

> *Almighty God, Ephesians 6:18 tells us to come before You with all prayers and petitions. So I am coming to You, asking You to bless my family and meet our needs. Lord, I need You all the time. Renew me by Your Spirit so that I am spiritually alert, sensitive to Your voice, and steadfast in faith. Thank You, Lord, for answering prayer. In Jesus' name, amen.*

These four components get God's attention, and when we approach Him in this way, we can be assured that He will answer.

EFFECTUAL, FERVENT PRAYER

Let's go back and review one of the scriptures I mentioned previously. James 5:16 reads, "Confess your trespasses to one another, and pray for one another, that you may be healed. The effective, fervent prayer of a righteous man avails much." In the latter part of this verse, the word that sticks out is "effective." My goal in writing this book isn't to say you've been praying all wrong. Rather, I hope to show you how to pray more effectively—how to take the promises of Scripture, target your petitions with clarity and authority, and present them before God in faith. When you pray this way, your faith is activated, and you step into the reality of what He has already spoken over your life. This is how you truly become what you believe.

Prayer is about more than meeting material needs. It is about seeing the power of God manifest in our situation and repositioning what is not in alignment with God's will for you, your family, and those you're interceding for. When we pray, we declare to everything that is contrary to the Word of God, everything that opposes the will of God, and everything that tries to deny the power of God: "Move out of the way because God is still on the throne." As Matthew 19:26 teaches, nothing is impossible for God.

Therefore, we pray not from a place of need but from a place of faith and trust. We must *believe* God for the answers to our prayers, and we must *believe* there is power through prayer. And again, for that power to be released, we must also be people of *faith*. A person of faith is one who realizes that while they are praying, God is moving. This is true even when they do not see things happening. We have to be people of faith to pray for the unseen.

The devil would just love for us to stay stuck. Our faith in almighty God should never waver or persuade us to stay in a place of doubt, fear, or double-mindedness. We have to trust God. We must acknowledge that He is real and has the last say in every area of our lives and in the lives of those we are covering in prayer. And we must pray with hope. Proverbs 13:12 says, "Hope deferred makes the heart sick." When we pray with hope, we keep our expectation alive and guard our hearts against discouragement.

Prayer is a weapon, but you won't know how beneficial your weapon is until you use it. If you are tired of nothing changing even though you prayed, this book is for you. If you are looking for God to move powerfully because you prayed, this book is for you. All the promises of God are yes in Him and amen (2 Cor. 1:20)—promises of peace, joy, provision, healing, and much more. Those promises are not distant hopes; they are your inheritance in Jesus. As you learn to pray God's Word with faith, you will be strengthened to believe His promises and walk in them fully. This is how you begin to truly become what you believe.

In the following pages, you will find specific topics—each selected prayerfully—along with scriptures related to those issues. The verses have been adapted into prayers that beckon the Lord to transform you. When you need God to move in a certain area of your life, find that topic and pray those scriptures. I also included a place for you to write your own scriptures to pray over your need. You can also use that space to journal what God reveals to you during your time of prayer. If the Lord gives you a word, a dream, or a vision, write it down. In time you will see how God answers your prayer or brings that word to pass in your life.

I hope that as you read this book, it becomes a seed—a seed that is planted in your life for a full harvest of answered prayers. As you see God moving, I pray you will plant that same seed of prayer in your family, your community, and beyond.

So get ready. Prepare to sound an alarm in the earth that God is still on the throne. Get ready to become what you believe!

PART I

BECOME ANCHORED IN GOD

Effective prayer is a byproduct of intimacy with God. The prayers in this section will guide you in developing a deep relationship with God that is rooted in His love.

CHAPTER 1

LONGING FOR A DEEPER RELATIONSHIP WITH GOD

EARLY IN ISRAEL's formation, Moses told the nation: "You shall love the LORD your God with all your heart, with all your soul, and with all your strength" (Deut. 6:5). This isn't just a command; it is our personal invitation to intimacy. God's desire is for us to crave His presence. He does not want us to "perform" for Him but to love Him.

In Psalm 23 we learn from King David that the Lord is our Shepherd. A good shepherd leads the flock out of harm's way and makes sure the sheep never go without. When we allow God to be our great Shepherd, we are saying that our relationship with Him is all we need. We surrender our lives to Him because we know He will direct our steps and that we can trust Him to make sure we have everything we need.

This is why David wrote: "The LORD is my shepherd; I shall not want. He makes me to lie down in green pastures; He leads me beside the still waters. He restores my soul; He leads me in the paths of righteousness for His name's sake" (Ps. 23:1–3). Because of his relationship with God, David knew He could trust Him to meet all his needs.

If we want the kind of confidence David had, we must deepen our relationship with the Lord. We must know Him intimately. As we talk to Him, He will respond. As we trust Him, He will be all we need. So rest in Him. He is your everything, and He is waiting to walk with you.

If you want a deeper relationship with God, use the following scriptures and prayers to declare God's Word over your life.

> You shall love the LORD your God with all your heart, with all your soul, and with all your strength.
> —DEUTERONOMY 6:5

Father, I thank You for giving me the best relationship I could ever have—with You. I love You, Lord God, with all my heart, with all my soul, and with all my strength.

The LORD is my shepherd; I shall not want. He makes me to lie down in green pastures; He leads me beside the still waters. He restores my soul; He leads me in the paths of righteousness for His name's sake.

—PSALM 23:1–3

Father God, I thank You for being my Shepherd. Because You are with me, I shall not want. Lack has no place in my life. You make me lie down in green pastures, so I declare rest, provision, and abundance are mine. You lead me beside still waters, and I proclaim peace, refreshing, and divine order in my soul. You restore my soul; therefore, I declare healing, wholeness, and renewal over my mind, will, and emotions. You lead me in the paths of righteousness, and I decree that I walk in holiness, in integrity, and in alignment with Your will, in Jesus' name.

However, you are not [living] in the flesh [controlled by the sinful nature] but in the Spirit, if in fact the Spirit of God lives in you [directing and guiding you]. But if anyone does not have the Spirit of Christ, he does not belong to Him [and is not a child of God].

—ROMANS 8:9, AMP

Lord Jesus, I honor and bless Your holy name. Thank You that I am not living in the flesh or bound by a sinful nature. Your Spirit lives in me, and because of that I am directed, guided, and empowered by You. Thank You for dwelling in me and claiming me as Your own child. I ask that those who do not yet know You would come to recognize their need for Your Spirit, so they may belong to You and walk in the fullness of life that only You can give.

Guide me in Your truth and teach me, for You are the God of my salvation; for You [and only You] I wait [expectantly] all the day long.

—PSALM 25:5, AMP

Father, I am honored by how You guide me in Your truth and teach me, for You are the God of my salvation. For You and only You do I wait with expectation all the day long.

The LORD is my rock, my fortress and my deliverer; my God is my rock, in whom I take refuge, my shield and the horn of my salvation, my stronghold.

—PSALM 18:2, NIV

Father, You are more than everything to me. Lord, You are my rock, my fortress, and my Deliverer. In You I take refuge, and I am secure. I honor You, Lord, for You are my shield that covers me, the horn of my salvation that gives me victory, and my stronghold that cannot be shaken.

I prayed to the LORD my God and confessed: "O Lord, you are a great and awesome God! You always fulfill your covenant and keep your promises of unfailing love to those who love you and obey your commands."

—DANIEL 9:4, NLT

Almighty God, I honor and bless Your name. I pray to the Lord my God and confess, "O Lord, You are a great and awesome God! You always fulfill Your covenant and keep Your promises of unfailing love to those who love You and obey Your commands."

On God my salvation and my glory rest; He is my rock of [unyielding] strength, my refuge is in God.

—PSALM 62:7, AMP

Father God, I have assurance that on You my salvation and my glory rest. You are my rock of strength. My refuge is in You.

&

....

....

....

....

CHAPTER 2

EXPERIENCING GOD'S LOVE

HAVE YOU EVER loved a perfect human being? No? I cannot say I have either. And guess what? God's love for us is not based on perfection. It's based on and rooted in His character! God *is* love, and He loves us unconditionally, sacrificially, and permanently. We know this because of what Paul wrote in Romans 5:8: "But God demonstrates His own love toward us, in that while we were still sinners, Christ died for us."

I hope you didn't miss the significance of those words. God knew all about us. He knew what we would do and why we would do it, and He still loved us. That's *real love.*

> **If you want to pray effectively and grow spiritually, start by receiving God's love.**

Because God is neither distant nor abstract, His love is not just a feeling; it's powerful. It redeems, restores, and breaks chains. It reflects who He is. His love matures in us, grows deep roots, and drives out fear. The Bible says that faith works through love (Gal. 5:6). So if you want to believe right and speak right, never yield to fear. As the Bible says, fear has no authority because God's perfect love casts it out (1 John 4:18).

If you want to pray effectively and grow spiritually, start by receiving God's love. Rest in the truth that, as John 3:16 says, God loved you so much that He sent His Son to die for you; God sent Him for each of us on this planet. Let that truth work its way deep into your soul, because once you know you're loved, you'll stop praying like a beggar and start praying like a child who knows their Father is good.

You are loved—not because you earned it, but because He chose to love you first.

> But God demonstrates His own love toward us, in that while
> we were still sinners, Christ died for us.
>
> —ROMANS 5:8

Father God, I thank You for demonstrating Your love toward me while I was still a sinner. You loved me so much that You sent Your Son to die for me. I know that is real love.

Now hope does not disappoint, because the love of God has been poured out in our hearts by the Holy Spirit who was given to us.

—ROMANS 5:5

I bless You, God, because in You, my hope is never disappointed. The love of God has been poured out into my heart by the gift of the Holy Spirit.

He who does not love does not know God, for God is love.

—1 JOHN 4:8

I hope because of Your love. I am steadfast in my journey because of Your love. I am blessed to know love, and that love is from You, Father.

God is love. When we take up permanent residence in a life of love, we live in God and God lives in us. This way, love has the run of the house, becomes at home and mature in us, so that we're free of worry on Judgment Day—our standing in the world is identical with Christ's. There is no room in love for fear. Well-formed love banishes fear. Since fear is crippling, a fearful life—fear of death, fear of judgment—is one not yet fully formed in love.

—1 JOHN 4:17–18, MSG

Lord God, to love You is to know that You are love. You have taken up permanent residence in my life. I live in You, God, and You live in me. Your love has the run of the house; it becomes at home, matures, and rules within me, so that I am free of worry on judgment day. My standing in this world is identical to Christ's. There is no room in love for fear. Well-formed love banishes fear, and in Jesus' name I declare that fear has no hold on me. I walk in confidence, boldness, and victory because Your perfect love reigns in me.

But God, being [so very] rich in mercy, because of His great and wonderful love with which He loved us.

—EPHESIANS 2:4, AMP

Father God, You are rich in mercy. Thank You for Your great and wonderful love toward me.

Now may the Lord direct your hearts into the love of God and into the patience of Christ.

—2 THESSALONIANS 3:5

Abba Father, I pray that You direct my heart into Your love and into the steadfast patience of Christ. Anchor my heart in Your love, and let it be my compass, my strength, and my constant pursuit.

If someone claims, "I know him well!" but doesn't keep his commandments, he's obviously a liar. His life doesn't match his words. But the one who keeps God's word is the person in whom we see God's mature love. This is the only way to be sure we're in God. Anyone who claims to be intimate with God ought to live the same kind of life Jesus lived.

—1 JOHN 2:5–6, MSG

Father, I declare that I know You, and I prove it by keeping Your commandments. My life won't contradict my confession—my walk will match my talk. I will keep Your Word in me, live in intimacy with You, and live the kind of life Jesus lived. Just as He walked in obedience and love, so I, too, will walk in obedience and love. This is the evidence that I am in You and that Your mature love is being formed in me.

Then Christ will make his home in your hearts as you trust in him. Your roots will grow down into God's love and keep you strong.

—EPHESIANS 3:17, NLT

Lord God, thank You for making Your home in my heart as I trust You. Lord, I pray Your roots will grow down into God's love and keep me strong!

For we have heard of your faith in Christ Jesus [how you lean on Him with absolute confidence in His power, wisdom, and goodness], and of the [unselfish] love which you have for all the saints (God's people).

—Colossians 1:4, amp

Lord Jesus, I honor and bless You. I have faith in You! I have absolute confidence in Your power, wisdom, and goodness. Because You live in me, I walk in unselfish love for all the saints—Your people.

This is real love—not that we loved God, but that he loved us and sent his Son as a sacrifice to take away our sins.

—1 John 4:10, nlt

Father, thank You for teaching me what real love is. It is not so much that I love God but that He loved me and sent His Son as a sacrifice to take away my sins. Thank You, Jesus, for loving me in such an awesome way!

છ

CHAPTER 3

ABIDING IN GOD'S PRESENCE

As I shared previously, prayer is a lifestyle. So often we expect God to answer us the moment we give Him our long list of demands, but very few of us have mastered abiding in God's presence and really waiting to hear what He has to say.

> **Abiding is not a onetime act; it must become a daily posture of surrender.**

To abide means to remain, dwell, and stay connected.[1] In John 15:4 Jesus calls us to abide in Him as He abides in us—because apart from Him, we can do nothing. Like a branch disconnected from its vine, we cannot bear fruit without God's presence and power flowing through us.

When we pray the Scriptures, we are abiding in Him, because we are openly declaring that God's Word lives in us, we believe it, and we will walk in obedience. As we do this, we become stronger and learn how to be truly victorious in life because abiding in Christ brings security, strength, and spiritual authority.

Abiding is not a onetime act; it must become a daily posture of surrender. We abide in Christ through His Spirit, who lives in us (1 John 4:13). Use these prayers to stay rooted, stay faithful, and stay in Him.

> Abide in Me, and I in you. As the branch cannot bear fruit of itself, unless it abides in the vine, neither can you, unless you abide in Me.
>
> —John 15:4

Jesus, I pray that I will continue to abide in You as You are abiding in me. I cannot produce fruit by myself, so I will remain connected to the vine and abide in You.

I write to you, fathers, because you have come to know (recognize, be conscious of, and understand) Him Who [has existed] from the beginning. I write to you, young men, because you are strong and vigorous, and the Word of God is [always] abiding in you (in your hearts), and you have been victorious over the wicked one.

—1 JOHN 2:14, AMPC

Lord, I have come to know, recognize, and understand that You existed from the beginning. Because of You I am strong and vigorous, and the Word of God is always abiding in my heart. Thank You, Jesus, for making me victorious over the wicked one.

He who dwells in the secret place of the Most High shall abide under the shadow of the Almighty.

—PSALM 91:1

Jesus, I thank You for causing me to dwell in the secret place of the Most High and to abide under the shadow of the Almighty. I declare that I live in Your presence, covered by Your power, and hidden in Your protection. Under Your shadow, I am safe and secure.

So, Jesus was saying to the Jews who had believed Him, "If you abide in My word [continually obeying My teachings and living in accordance with them, then] you are truly My disciples."

—JOHN 8:31, AMP

Father, I bless and honor You. And just as Jesus said to those Jews who believed, so You say to me: If I abide in Your Word, continually obeying Your teachings and living in accordance with them, then I am truly Your disciple. In Jesus' name, I declare that I remain rooted in Your Word, walk in obedience to Your teachings, and bear witness that I follow You.

If you abide in Me, and My words abide in you, you will ask what you desire, and it shall be done for you.

—JOHN 15:7

Almighty God, I know if I abide in You and Your words abide in me, I can ask You what I desire, and it shall be done for me.

I have written to you who are God's children because you know
the Father. I have written to you who are mature in the faith
because you know Christ, who existed from the beginning. I
have written to you who are young in the faith because you are
strong. God's word lives in your hearts, and you have won your
battle with the evil one.

—1 JOHN 2:14 , NLT

*Father, I thank You because I am Your child. I know the Father
and am maturing in the faith because I know Christ, who existed
from the beginning. Although young in faith, I am strong because
God's Word lives in my heart, and I have won the battle with the
evil one.*

He who believes in the Son has everlasting life; and he who
does not believe the Son shall not see life, but the wrath of God
abides on him.

—JOHN 3:36

*Father, I abide in You because I believe in the Son, who has ever-
lasting life, and I know he who does not believe the Son shall not
see life, but the wrath of God abides on him.*

When you obey my commandments, you remain in my love, just
as I obey my Father's commandments and remain in his love.

—JOHN 15:10, NLT

*Lord Jesus, my prayer is that I will continue to abide in You. I
pray I shall obey Your commandments and remain in Your love,
just as You obey Your Father's commandments and remain in
His love.*

But you have received the Holy Spirit, and he lives within you,
in your hearts, so that you don't need anyone to teach you what
is right. For he teaches you all things, and he is the Truth, and
no liar; and so, just as he has said, you must live in Christ, never
to depart from him.

—1 JOHN 2:27, TLB

*Father, I bless and honor You! Thank You for giving me the Holy
Spirit, who lives inside me and teaches me all things. He is the*

truth and not a liar! So I must live in Christ and never depart from Him.

By this we know that we abide in Him, and He in us, because He has given us of His Spirit.

—1 JOHN 4:13

Lord, I abide in You, and You are in me because You have given me Your Spirit.

But Judah shall abide forever, and Jerusalem from generation to generation.

—JOEL 3:20

Father, I pray my praise shall abide forever, from generation to generation.

But he who looks carefully into the perfect law, the law of liberty, and faithfully abides by it, not having become a [careless] listener who forgets but an active doer [who obeys], he will be blessed and favored by God in what he does [in his life of obedience].

—JAMES 1:25, AMP

Lord God, I thank You for Your Word, and I will faithfully abide in it. I will not be a careless listener who forgets Your truth but an active doer who obeys. Thank You for blessing and favoring me because of my obedience.

೮೨

CHAPTER 4

LIVING IN GOD'S
KINGDOM PROMISES

As we deepen and strengthen our lifestyle of prayer, we can reach a point of doubt when we view our experiences from the perspective of the world and not of the kingdom. Beloved, you and I are *kingdom* citizens. We are *kingdom ambassadors*. The kingdom of God is not a future destination. It is a present reality for all who submit to the lordship of Jesus Christ.

> **When we pray for the kingdom to come, we invite God to rule in our hearts, homes, schools, workplaces, and communities.**

When we pray "Your kingdom come" (Matt. 6:10), we are aligning ourselves with God's divine authority and rule in the earth. Praying about the kingdom is a call to righteousness, peace, and joy in the Holy Spirit (Rom. 14:17). It shifts our focus from personal gain to kingdom purpose. We have a divine purpose that will allow us to have the benefits of Jesus' kingdom here on earth. Therefore, we begin to take hold of the responsibility to advance God's agenda and to teach those all over the world the Lord's truth.

When we pray for the kingdom to come, we invite God to rule in our hearts, homes, schools, workplaces, and communities. As His kingdom is established in your life, you will become a reflection of the culture of heaven. Your thoughts, words, and actions will be guided and governed by the Holy Spirit, and you will reap the benefits of being called His own.

> But seek first the kingdom of God and His righteousness, and all these things shall be added to you.
> —Matthew 6:33

Lord, I bless and honor You. I seek first Your kingdom and Your righteousness, and all these things shall be added to me.

And my speech and my preaching were not with persuasive words of human wisdom, but in demonstration of the Spirit and of power.

—1 Corinthians 2:4

Father, I thank You that the way I speak and preach are not with persuasive words of human wisdom but in the demonstration of Your Spirit and power.

Your kingdom is an everlasting kingdom, and Your dominion endures throughout all generations.

—Psalm 145:13

Jesus, I give You honor and glory because Your kingdom is an everlasting kingdom and Your dominion lasts throughout every generation. In the name of Jesus, I declare that Your kingdom rules in me! Your everlasting kingdom is what I seek first.

For the kingdom is the Lord's, and He rules over the nations.

—Psalm 22:28

Lord God Almighty, I declare that the kingdom is Yours, and You rule over the nations.

That your daily lives should not embarrass God but bring joy to him who invited you into his Kingdom to share his glory.

—1 Thessalonians 2:12, tlb

Abba Father, I pray that my daily life won't embarrass You but bring You joy. Thank You for inviting me into the kingdom to share in Your glory!

For the kingdom of God is not eating and drinking, but righteousness and peace and joy in the Holy Spirit.

—Romans 14:17

Jesus, I thank You for the revelation that the kingdom of God is not eating and drinking but righteousness, peace, and joy in the Holy Spirit.

The Lord has made the heavens his throne; from there he rules over everything there is.

—PSALM 103:19, TLB

Father, I bless Your name, for You have made the heavens Your throne, and from there You rule over everything there is. I thank You that You reign over my life, and I rest in the power of Your rule.

They shall speak of the glory of Your kingdom, and talk of Your power.

—PSALM 145:11, AMP

Father, I pray that I shall speak the glory of Your kingdom and talk of Your power.

Your kingdom come. Your will be done on earth as it is in heaven.

—MATTHEW 6:10

Almighty God, Your kingdom come. Your will be done, on earth as it is in heaven!

But if I am casting out demons by the Spirit of God, then the Kingdom of God has arrived among you.

—MATTHEW 12:28, NLT

My Father and my God, I thank You that when Your Spirit works through me, it is evidence that the kingdom of God is here. Let Your kingdom advance in me and through me, bringing freedom, deliverance, and victory everywhere You send me.

And do not lead us into temptation, but deliver us from the evil one. For Yours is the kingdom and the power and the glory forever. Amen.

—MATTHEW 6:13

Abba Father, I thank You that You do not lead us into temptation but deliver us from the evil one—for Yours is the kingdom and the power and the glory forever. Amen.

Again, the kingdom of heaven is like treasure hidden in a field, which a man found and hid; and for joy over it he goes and sells all that he has and buys that field.

—MATTHEW 13:44

Father, I honor and thank You for teaching me that the kingdom of heaven is like a treasure hidden in a field, which a man found and hid, and for joy over the treasure sold all he had and bought that field. Lord Jesus, You are my greatest treasure, worth more than anything this world can offer. With joy I surrender all that I have to gain You and Your kingdom. Let my heart value You above all else and let my life reflect the joy of finding true riches in You.

೮ာ

CHAPTER 5

WORSHIPPING IN SPIRIT AND TRUTH

WORSHIP IS MORE than a song; it's a lifestyle of surrender and adoration. John 4:24 says that God seeks those who worship Him in spirit and in truth. Worship invites God's presence and shifts our perspective. It lifts our eyes from problems to the One who reigns over them.

> **Worship transforms your heart and creates space for miracles.**

Worship in prayer sounds like this: "Lord, You are holy, worthy, and faithful. I bless Your name. I give You glory and honor, now and into eternity." You don't have to feel good to worship because worship brings you into the joy and presence of God.

Let your prayers be filled with thanksgiving and reverence because worship transforms your heart and creates space for miracles.

> God is Spirit, and those who worship Him must worship in spirit and truth.
>
> —JOHN 4:24

Father God, You are Spirit, and I worship You in spirit and truth.

> Give unto the LORD the glory due to His name; worship the LORD in the beauty of holiness.
>
> —PSALM 29:2

Abba Father, You are holy, and I give You the glory due to Your name. I worship You in the beauty of holiness.

> Now we know that God does not hear sinners; but if anyone is a worshiper of God and does His will, He hears him.
>
> —JOHN 9:31

Father, I worship You and do Your will. Thank You for hearing me.

"And now, behold, I have brought the firstfruits of the land which you, O Lord, have given me." Then you shall set it before the Lord your God, and worship before the Lord your God.

—Deuteronomy 26:10

Jesus, I honor and bless You with my best. I bring You the first of what You have given me: my time, my talent, my finances. I set them before You, Lord, and worship before You.

But worship only the Lord, who brought you out of Egypt with great strength and a powerful arm. Bow down to him alone, and offer sacrifices only to him.

—2 Kings 17:36, nlt

Lord God, I worship You who brings me out of places of bondage with great strength and Your powerful arm. I bow to You alone in worship.

Give to the Lord the glory due His name; bring an offering, and come before Him. Oh, worship the Lord in the beauty of holiness!

—1 Chronicles 16:29

God, I give You the glory that is due Your name. I give You an offering, and I worship You in the beauty of holiness.

There's no one quite like you among the gods, O Lord, and nothing to compare with your works. All the nations you made are on their way, ready to give honor to you, O Lord, ready to put your beauty on display, parading your greatness, and the great things you do—God, you're the one, there's no one but you!

—Psalm 86:9–10, msg

Father, there is nobody like You, and nothing can compare to Your works. You made the nation and everyone in it, and I will honor You, Your greatness, and the great things only You can do!

As he listens, his secret thoughts will be laid bare, and he will
fall down on his knees and worship God, declaring that God is
really there among you.

—1 Corinthians 14:25, tlb

Lord God, lay bare my secret thoughts as I listen to Your voice.
You are holy and none can compare to You, yet You are with me.
I fall down and worship You.

"Fear God," he shouted. "Give glory to him. For the time has
come when he will sit as judge. Worship him who made the
heavens, the earth, the sea, and all the springs of water."

—Revelation 14:7, nlt

Lord, I give You glory. You are the judge, and You made the
heavens, the earth, the sea, and all the springs of water. I give my
life back to You in worship. I glorify You and all that You have
done. I know that I am helpless and cannot save myself. Therefore,
I need You, and I worship You.

My firstfruit is my worship; my acknowledgment of Your truth
is my worship! When situations try to distract me, I worship You.
When enemies continue to attack me, I will push myself to wor-
ship You! My worship is not based on my feelings. It is based on
my relationship with You. My understanding of true intimacy,
love, and even my understanding of who You are in my life comes
from a place of worship. If I do not make a sound, but my mind
is on You, this is my worship! If I sing, this is my worship. If I am
still in Your presence, knowing You are with me, this is my wor-
ship. Thank You, Lord.

ଚ୍ଚ

CHAPTER 6

LIVING THE ABUNDANT LIFE GOD PROMISED

L IFE IS BUT a vapor, and it would be a shame not to experience the life that God wants for us because we lack the ability to pray correctly. According to John 10:10 Jesus came so that we may have life, and that life is to be representative of His abundance. When we pray, we give breath to purpose. Our words speak life that awakens people to the fullness of God's design.

> **In Christ, we are promised a life where we can live in joy, power, and peace.**

The prayers we are declaring in this book speak blessings, longevity, health, and purpose over ourselves and those we love. This chapter is specifically for us to know exactly what Psalm 118:17 declares: "I shall not die, but live, and declare the works of the LORD."

My brother and sister, you and I are not merely survivors. Because we are in Christ, we are promised a life where we can live in joy, power, and peace. These next prayers align us with serving faithfully, living fully, and loving deeply. Each breath counts because we are on earth for a divine reason and purpose. Speak life.

For God so loved the world that He gave His only begotten Son, that whoever believes in Him should not perish but have everlasting life.

—John 3:16

Lord God, thank You for so loving the world that You gave Your only begotten Son, that whoever believes in Him should not perish but have everlasting life. Because I believe in Him, I will not perish but have everlasting life. I declare that eternal life is mine

*through Jesus, and I will live each day in the power of Your love
and the victory He purchased on the cross.*

Holding fast the word of life, so that I may rejoice in the day of
Christ that I have not run in vain or labored in vain.

—PHILIPPIANS 2:16

*Almighty God, I will not run this race in vain. I will hold fast
to the Word of life and rejoice in the day of Christ. I declare life
over every place that seems dry and dead. I shall have a wonderful, prosperous, abundant life. My territory is already enlarged
because of the greatness in my life!*

His divine power has given to us all things that pertain to life
and godliness, through the knowledge of Him who called us by
glory and virtue.

—2 PETER 1:3

*Father God, Your divine power has given me all things that per-
tain to life and godliness, through the knowledge of Him who
called me by glory and virtue. Lord, I thank You that through
knowing You, I walk in provision, wisdom, and strength. I declare
that I lack nothing but have all I need to live a life that glorifies
You and fulfill my calling.*

ಜ

PART II

BECOME BOLD IN PRAYER

Prayer is powerful when it is done with confidence, authority, and faith. This section will help you align with God's Word so you can pray boldly, declaring His truth over every situation.

CHAPTER 7

PRAYING WITH AUTHORITY

WHEN IT COMES to prayer, many believers struggle with the idea of being in authority. This is why it is essential to know that when we pray, we do not pray from the position of a beggar. We are sons and daughters of God with kingdom positioning and authority. Jesus said in Luke 10:19, "Behold, I give you the authority...over all the power of the enemy."

One of the first steps you must take in prayer is knowing that your authority is shaped by your identity in Christ. Once you understand that you have authority in Christ, you will begin to tap into your kingdom access. When we are in position to pray with authority, our prayers become commands. We do not negotiate with the enemy or merely suggest that he leave. We take a stance that becomes a command—we *command* that he flees. We do not merely hope for a breakthrough or deliverance; we *declare* by *faith* that breakthrough and deliverance are our portion.

Matthew 18:18 reminds us that what we bind and loose on earth must be bound or loosed in heaven. We exercise that authority by the Word we speak, the power of the blood—which seals the Word—and the *faith* we choose to walk in. (See chapter 10.)

> **Your authority is shaped by your identity in Christ.**

I challenge you to walk in the truth that heaven backs your prayers. When we speak healing, release peace, or decree restoration, we do so not in our own strength but in the matchless and mighty name of Jesus. Because of Him we are seated in heavenly places, and we can boldly take authority in His name, knowing that heaven will respond to our prayers.

> Be strong in the Lord and in his mighty power. Put on all of God's armor so that you will be able to stand firm against all strategies of the devil. For we are not fighting against flesh-and-blood enemies, but against evil rulers and authorities of

the unseen world, against mighty powers in this dark world, and against evil spirits in the heavenly places.

Therefore, put on every piece of God's armor so you will be able to resist the enemy in the time of evil. Then after the battle you will still be standing firm. Stand your ground, putting on the belt of truth and the body armor of God's righteousness. For shoes, put on the peace that comes from the Good News so that you will be fully prepared. In addition to all of these, hold up the shield of faith to stop the fiery arrows of the devil. Put on salvation as your helmet, and take the sword of the Spirit, which is the word of God.

Pray in the Spirit at all times and on every occasion. Stay alert and be persistent in your prayers for all believers everywhere.

And pray for me, too. Ask God to give me the right words so I can boldly explain God's mysterious plan that the Good News is for Jews and Gentiles alike. I am in chains now, still preaching this message as God's ambassador. So pray that I will keep on speaking boldly for him, as I should.

—EPHESIANS 6:10–20, NLT

Father, I take authority in this atmosphere and declare that I will be strong in You and in Your mighty power. I put on Your armor so I can stand firm against the strategies of the devil. Thank You for reminding me that I am not fighting with flesh and blood but against evil rulers that I cannot see, mighty powers in this dark world, and evil spirits in heavenly places.

Thank You for giving me every piece of armor I need to resist the enemy in the time of evil. With You on my side, I will be standing firm after the battle! I take authority and stand my ground! I put on the belt of truth and the body armor of God's righteousness. The shoes I wear are those of peace, and they come from the good news that I will be fully prepared. I also add the shield of my faith to stop all fiery darts of the devil. I put on my helmet of salvation and the sword of the Spirit, which is the Word of God. Lord, I pray in the Spirit all the time and during every occasion.

Lord, thank You for keeping me alert and persistent in prayer for believers everywhere. Thank You for covering me and giving me the right words so I can boldly explain Your mysterious plan to people from all walks of life. Although life may have me in chains momentarily, I take authority over it and shall speak boldly as I should.

Look, I have given you authority over all the power of the enemy, and you can walk among snakes and scorpions and crush them. Nothing will injure you.

—LUKE 10:19, NLT

Jesus, I thank You for giving me authority and power over every enemy! I can walk among the snakes and scorpions in my way, crush them, and know I will not get hurt.

And Jesus came and spoke to them, saying, "All authority has been given to Me in heaven and on earth."

—MATTHEW 28:18

Lord Jesus, all authority has been given to You in heaven and on earth. I submit to Your authority and stand in the power You have given me to trample on the enemy (Luke 10:19). In You I am more than a conqueror (Rom. 8:37). I walk in victory through Your name.

For I have never spoken on My own initiative or authority, but the Father Himself who sent Me has given Me a commandment regarding what to say and what to speak.

—JOHN 12:49, AMP

Lord Jesus, I bless and honor You! You never spoke out of Your own initiative or authority, and neither will I. The Father Himself who sent You gave You a commandment regarding what to say and what to speak, and I trust that He will do the same with me. He will put His words in my mouth and use me to declare His will in the earth.

As You have given Him authority over all flesh, that He should give eternal life to as many as You have given Him.

—JOHN 17:2

Lord God, You gave Jesus authority over all flesh that He should give eternal life to as many as You have given Him—and that includes me!

Then they were all amazed and spoke among themselves, saying, "What a word this is! For with authority and power He commands the unclean spirits, and they come out."

—Luke 4:36

Father, just as unclean spirits had to come out when You commanded them to leave, so You have given me authority that they have to obey, So demons must flee when I command them to go in Your name.

He gives power to the weak, and to those who have no might He increases strength.

—Isaiah 40:29

Father, I bless Your holy name! I thank You for giving power to the weak and increasing the strength of those who have no might! You alone have the power and authority to increase strength!

Everyone must submit to governing authorities. For all authority comes from God, and those in positions of authority have been placed there by God.

—Romans 13:1, nlt

Father, help me respect governing authorities, for all authority comes from You and was put in place by You.

I may seem to be boasting more than I should about my authority over you—authority to help you, not to hurt you—but I shall make good every claim.

—2 Corinthians 10:8, tlb

Lord God, I am reminded through Your Word that the spiritual authority You have placed over me is there to help me, not to hurt me. Every good gift comes from You!

Not because we do not have authority, but to make ourselves an example of how you should follow us.

—2 Thessalonians 3:9

Dear God, please help me remember that I am to follow Your spiritual authority, not try to proclaim my own, as I make myself an example of how others are to follow You.

The first thing I want you to do is pray. Pray every way you know how, for everyone you know. Pray especially for rulers and their governments to rule well so we can be quietly about our business of living simply, in humble contemplation. This is the way our Savior God wants us to live.

—1 Timothy 2:2, msg

Father, I pray that the authority You trust me to carry and the rule I exercise may be done well, and that my life may be quiet, simple, and humble. For this is the way You want me to live. Amen!

You must teach these things and encourage the believers to do them. You have the authority to correct them when necessary, so don't let anyone disregard what you say.

—Titus 2:15, nlt

Today, God, help me teach and encourage others. I realize I have the authority to correct, and I shall do so, but I pray that my words are valued.

I will give you the keys (authority) of the kingdom of heaven; and whatever you bind [forbid, declare to be improper and unlawful] on earth will have [already] been bound in heaven, and whatever you loose [permit, declare lawful] on earth will have [already] been loosed in heaven.

—Matthew 16:19, amp

Father, I thank You for giving me the keys of authority to the kingdom of heaven. Whatever I bind or declare to be wrong on earth is already bound in heaven, and whatever I loose or permit on earth is already loosed in heaven.

After these things I saw another angel coming down from heaven, having great authority, and the earth was illuminated with his glory.

—Revelation 18:1

Lord, I honor and bless Your name for it is You who has great authority, and the earth is illuminated by Your glory!

ॐ

....

....

....

....

CHAPTER 8

SEEKING GREATER VISION

WHERE THERE IS no vision, the people perish (Prov. 29:18). Prayer helps clarify purpose and align you with God's vision for your life. Vision gives direction, focus, and hope. As you pray, ask God to open your spiritual eyes so you can see what He sees.

God can give you clarity beyond your current reality. When you accept this, dreaming will be easy again. Vision doesn't always come in a flash; it's often revealed step by step. Stay prayerful and obedient. Write the vision (Hab. 2:2), speak it, and pray over it until it manifests. With God-given vision you won't just be busy; you will be purposeful.

> He sought God in the days of Zechariah, who had understanding in the visions of God; and as long as he sought the LORD, God made him prosper.
>
> —2 CHRONICLES 26:5

Father God, give me vision and help me understand what You reveal. I praise and thank You for insight and understanding. Help me embrace Your vision and seek Your direction so that I may prosper.

Ask God to open your spiritual eyes so you can see what He sees.

> After these things the word of the LORD came to Abram in a vision, saying, "Do not be afraid, Abram. I am your shield, your exceedingly great reward."
>
> —GENESIS 15:1

Heavenly Father, You gave Abraham a vision to reveal that he should not be afraid. Give me a vision to discern Your will. I thank You for reminding me that You are my shield and my exceedingly great reward.

Then the LORD answered me and said: "Write the vision and make it plain on tablets, that he may run who reads it."

—HABAKKUK 2:2

Father God, I heard Your answer to me: Write the vision and make it plain on tablets so that he may run who reads it. I shall see what You say through Your Word! Your vision for me is to prosper. It is for me to succeed in life, and I have to write it down to read and run with it!

The vision of the evenings and the mornings which has been told [to you] is true. But keep the vision a secret, for it has to do with many days in the now distant future.

—DANIEL 8:26, AMP

Lord, I bless and thank You for the visions You reveal in the evening and in the morning. You are the God who reveals what I need for today and what is appointed for the future. I thank You that the vision is true, and I trust You to unfold it in Your perfect timing.

> **Vision doesn't always come in a flash;
> it's often revealed step by step.**

And it shall come to pass in the last days, says God, that I will pour out of My Spirit on all flesh; your sons and your daughters shall prophesy, your young men shall see visions, your old men shall dream dreams.

—ACTS 2:17

Father, I bless You for pouring out Your Spirit on all flesh. I decree and declare that sons and daughters shall rise and prophesy with boldness. I declare that young men will see visions from heaven, and old men will dream dreams. I proclaim that Your Spirit is moving with power across generations, unlocking gifts, releasing revelation, and fulfilling Your Word in our time.

For all the land which you see I give to you and your descendants forever.

—GENESIS 13:15

Almighty God, I thank You for opening my eyes to see the land You are giving me. I bless You for the inheritance You have promised— not only to me but to my descendants forever. I declare that what You have shown me, I will possess. I receive it by faith, and I trust that Your covenant promise will endure through generations.

And he who sees Me sees Him who sent Me.

—John 12:45

Dear God, I know that when I see You, I see who sent You! Open my eyes to see more of who You are and let my life reflect that revelation to others.

I know your deeds. See, I have set before you an open door which no one is able to shut, for you have a little power, and have kept My word, and have not renounced or denied My name.

—Revelation 3:8, amp

Father, I honor and bless You, and I see the open door You have set before me that no one can shut. I have no power, but I have kept Your Word, and You cannot be rejected or denied.

After these things the word of the Lord came to Abram in a vision, saying, "Do not be afraid, Abram. I am your shield, your exceedingly great reward."

—Genesis 15:1

Lord, I thank You that You are the God who gives vision. Just as Your Word came to Abram in a vision, You come to me and reveal Your plans. I will not be afraid because You are my shield and my exceedingly great reward. Thank You for the visions You release that lead, guide, and secure my future.

In a dream, a vision of the night [one may hear God's voice], when deep sleep falls on men while slumbering upon the bed.

—Job 33:15, amp

Lord, I thank You for speaking to me in my dreams and through visions!

To open their eyes, in order to turn them from darkness to light,
and from the power of Satan to God, that they may receive forgiveness of sins and an inheritance among those who are sancti-
fied by faith in Me.

—Acts 26:18

*Almighty God, when I open my eyes, my sight turns from darkness
to light and away from the power of Satan to God. Lord, I thank
You for forgiving me for my sins and providing an inheritance to
me because of my faith.*

℘

....

....

....

....

CHAPTER 9

TRUSTING GOD FOR OPEN DOORS, WINDOWS, AND GATES

WINDOWS, DOORS, AND gates represent divine access points in the spirit. In prayer you can open what has been closed and close what should not touch you as God's child. Malachi 3:10 says that God will open the windows of heaven and pour out blessings on those who tithe. In Revelation 3:8, Jesus declares, "See, I have set before you an open door, and no one can shut it." Because we plead the blood of Jesus over our lives when we pray, we can be confident of victory over the enemy.

When we pray, we should ask God to open divine doors of opportunity, favor, and increase. Pray that God will send us intentional relationships that align with open doors, windows, and gates. As we pray, we will break ties with confusion, fear, and delay. I want you to determine in your heart and mind that you will walk through every open door God has for you and that your gates will be called "praise"! There is power in spiritual positioning, so be alert, ready, and aligned.

> It was the six-hundredth year of Noah's life, in the second month, on the seventeenth day of the month that it happened: all the underground springs erupted and all the windows of Heaven were thrown open. Rain poured for forty days and forty nights.
> —Genesis 7:11–12, msg

> **In prayer you can open what has been closed and close what should not touch you as God's child.**

Dear Lord, open every window, door, and gate in my life with Your unlimited favor, abundance, and grace. I declare this is done. I pray that just as You did for Noah, You would throw open the windows of heaven and pour out Your Spirit on me. Do such amazing things that people will marvel over them.

Stand in the gate of the LORD's house, and proclaim there this word, and say, "Hear the word of the LORD, all you of Judah who enter in at these gates to worship the LORD!"

—JEREMIAH 7:2

Father God, I stand in the gate of Your house and boldly proclaim Your Word. I declare, "Hear the word of the Lord, all who enter these gates to worship Him." I will praise You, God, for You alone are worthy. I thank You for opening doors that no one can shut and blessing all who believe in Your Son!

But he commanded the skies to open; he opened the doors of heaven.

—PSALM 78:23, NLT

Abba Father, I thank You for commanding the skies to open and for opening the doors of heaven. You alone can do such an awesome and mighty thing. I praise You, God, for Your sovereignty, power, and glory. There is no one else like You.

So you also, when you see all these things, know that it is near—at the doors!

—MATTHEW 24:33

Lord, I thank You that the hour of Your visitation is near. You are opening those doors!

Suddenly, there was a massive earthquake, and the prison was shaken to its foundations. All the doors immediately flew open, and the chains of every prisoner fell off!

—ACTS 16:26, NLT

Father, I thank You for suddenly shaking things in my life—for opening doors and breaking chains!

For a great and effective door has opened to me, and there are many adversaries.

—1 CORINTHIANS 16:9

Jesus, I thank You for the great and effective door You have opened for me despite the many adversaries.

And I also say to you that you are Peter, and on this rock I will build My church, and the gates of Hades shall not prevail against it.

—MATTHEW 16:18

Almighty God, I decree and declare that Your church has been built on the rock, and the gates of hell will not prevail against it.

Open the gates to all who are righteous; allow the faithful to enter.

—ISAIAH 26:2, NLT

God Almighty, I thank You for opening the gates for the faithful to enter. I am faithful, and I will enter.

Blessed (happy, prosperous, to be admired) are those who wash their robes [in the blood of Christ by believing and trusting in Him—the righteous who do His commandments], so that they may have the right to the tree of life, and may enter by the gates into the city.

—REVELATION 22:14, AMP

Lord Jesus, I thank You that I am washed in Your blood and made righteous through faith in You. Because I believe and trust in You, I have the right to the tree of life and access through the gates of the city. I declare that I am blessed, happy, prosperous, and admired, for I belong to You.

Open the gates to everyone, for all may enter in who love the LORD.

—ISAIAH 26:2, TLB

Almighty God, I thank You that the gates are open for everyone who loves You!

Lift up your heads, O you gates! And be lifted up, you everlasting doors! And the King of glory shall come in.

—PSALM 24:7

Father, I lift my head to You and go through doors that are always open. As these doors are open, I know that Your glory shall come in. I praise You for the blessings of knowing You.

Go through his open gates with great thanksgiving; enter his courts with praise. Give thanks to him and bless his name.
—PSALM 100:4, TLB

I enter Your gates with thanksgiving and Your courts with praise. I give glory to You for the open gates You have set before me. As I enter through them, I thank You and bless Your name, for You are good and worthy of all praise.

Save me, so that I can praise you publicly before all the people at Jerusalem's gates and rejoice that you have rescued me.
—PSALM 9:14, TLB

Thank You, Jesus, for saving me. I praise You publicly and rejoice because You have rescued me.

PRAYER FOR OPEN DOORS

O Lord, I thank You for this day that You have made (Ps. 118:24). I rejoice and am glad in it. I thank You for Your faithfulness, mercy, and grace upon my life and family.

Father, thank You for the gift of abundant life in Christ Jesus.

Lord Jesus, I want open doors in my life and destiny. Surprise me this week, in Jesus' name.

Doors and opportunities, open unto me, in the name of Jesus. Lost opportunities, resurrect by fire, in the name of Jesus.

O God, arise, and single me out for uncommon success, in the name of Jesus.

Open my eyes, O Lord, that I may behold wondrous things, in the name of Jesus. Shake out of my life anything that is bringing shame to me, in the name of Jesus.

Anointing for promotion and fruitfulness, fall upon my life, in the name of Jesus.

Lord Jesus, help me in every situation in which I find myself, in the name of Jesus.

Every power that is closing the doors of my happiness, O Lord, frustrate them, in Jesus' name.

Supernatural breakthroughs that have never happened in my family, locate me, in Jesus' name.

In all areas of my life, I will experience the power of Your divine visitation, in Jesus' name.

O Lord, meet me at the point of my need, in Jesus' name. Restore the wasted years of my life, in Jesus' name. I apply the blood of Jesus against all my problems, in the name of Jesus.

O God, arise and let my joy be full, in the name of Jesus. Let every impossible situation become possible this month, in Jesus' name.

A BEDTIME PRAYER FOR OPEN DOORS

Men and women shall arise and begin to bless me and my family, in Jesus' name.

I shall find favors from unusual quarters, in Jesus' name. Holy Ghost, open by thunder every door shut against fruitfulness in my life, in Jesus' name.

There shall be an outpouring of God's blessings upon my life and household in Jesus' name.

O Lord, shut every evil door that has been opened in my life, marriage, finances, health, and so on, in Jesus' name.

Father, where my destiny has been satanically hindered, loose it and bring it into full manifestation.

Lord, open all the good doors that were shut by household wickedness, in Jesus' name.

I decree, declare, and proclaim that the doors of heavenly treasures are open permanently to me, in Jesus' name.

Lord, destroy with Your fire anything that causes Your promises for my life to fail, in the name of Jesus.

Father, put to shame whoever has come under an oath or vow to block the flow of good things in my life, in Jesus' name.

May the voice of marine witchcraft closing my doors of fruitfulness shut up and roast, in the name of Jesus.

By the blood of Jesus, I cancel dreams of anti-blessings, anti-favor, and anti-success, in Jesus' name.

Let the hand of the Almighty God push me to the point of breakthrough, in Jesus' name.

O Lord, the delay feels like too much. Please answer me now, in the name of Jesus.

Everything done to spoil my joy, be destroyed, in the name of Jesus.

Any satanic parasite attached to the open doors over my life, Holy Ghost fire, flush them away, in the name of Jesus.

Whoever or whatever is rebelling against the open doors concerning my destiny, fall down and die, in Jesus' name.

All marks of impossibility, be removed by fire, in Jesus' name.

Anything in my life that does not want me to finish well, come out now, in Jesus' name.

Father, I receive Your deliverance from all past failures and setbacks, in Jesus' name.

&

CHAPTER 10

APPLYING THE BLOOD OF JESUS

THE BLOOD OF Jesus is the most powerful force in the universe. It redeems, heals, protects, cleanses, and grants access to the Father. Revelation 12:11 declares, "They overcame him by the blood of the Lamb and by the word of their testimony." Plead the blood over your life, family, home, and mind. The blood silences the voice of the accuser. He can no longer come and make us feel as though we are not forgiven, cleansed, or covered. Beloved, there is no sin too deep or any battle too strong that the blood of Jesus cannot handle. Let the blood of Jesus be your defense and your declaration.

Meditate on that power as you pray God's Word over your life:

> But if we walk in the light as He is in the light, we have fellowship with one another, and the blood of Jesus Christ His Son cleanses us from all sin.
>
> —1 John 1:7

> *Lord God, I thank You that if I walk in the light as You are in the light, I have fellowship with other believers, and the blood of Jesus Christ cleanses me from all sin.*

> Grace to you and peace from Him who is and who was and who is to come, and from the seven Spirits who are before His throne, and from Jesus Christ, the faithful witness, the firstborn from the dead, and the ruler over the kings of the earth. To Him who loved us and washed us from our sins in His own blood.
>
> —Revelation 1:4–6

> *Abba Father, I lift my voice in gratitude for Jesus Christ, the Faithful Witness, the firstborn from the dead, and the ruler over the kings of the earth. May I always lift high the One who loves me and has washed me from my sins with His own blood. May*

my life continually honor You, Jesus, and may I forever proclaim
Your rule, victory, and matchless love.

But now you have been united with Christ Jesus. Once you
were far away from God, but now you have been brought near
to him through the blood of Christ.

—Ephesians 2:13, nlt

Lord, I bless You with every fiber of my being for You have united
me with Christ Jesus. Once I was far away from Him, but now,
through the power of His precious blood, I have been brought near.
Thank You for drawing me close and allowing me to fellowship
with You through Jesus Christ.

For God presented Jesus as the sacrifice for sin. People are
made right with God when they believe that Jesus sacrificed
his life, shedding his blood. This sacrifice shows that God was
being fair when he held back and did not punish those who
sinned in times past.

—Romans 3:25, nlt

Father God, I thank You for presenting Jesus as the sacrifice
for sin. By His blood I am made right with You. I rejoice in the
eternal security and salvation that come through the Lamb who
was slain. Because of Jesus all who believe in Him are forgiven,
redeemed, and promised everlasting life with You. I bless You for
the power of the cross and the victory won through His shed blood.

But now [at this very moment] in Christ Jesus you who once
were [so very] far away [from God] have been brought near by
the blood of Christ.

—Ephesians 2:13, amp

Father, I bless You for this very moment. I realize that I was
once distant from You, but the blood of Jesus brought me closer.
Thank You.

Pray for us. We have no doubts about what we're doing or
why, but it's hard going and we need your prayers. All we
care about is living well before God. Pray that we may be
together soon.

May God, who puts all things together, makes all things whole, who made a lasting mark through the sacrifice of Jesus, the sacrifice of blood that sealed the eternal covenant, who led Jesus, our Great Shepherd, up and alive from the dead, now put you together, provide you with everything you need to please him, make us into what gives him most pleasure, by means of the sacrifice of Jesus, the Messiah. All glory to Jesus forever and always! Oh, yes, yes, yes.

—Hebrews 13:20–21, msg

Almighty God, I thank You for the power of prayer. When I do not know what I am doing or even why I am doing it, Your prayers help me live right before You. You put things together, make them whole, and leave a lasting mark because of Jesus' sacrifice. The sacrifice of His blood that seals the lasting promise: The Great Shepherd is alive. Through Him I have everything I need. I declare glory to God forever!

A PRAYER TO PLEAD THE POWER OF THE BLOOD

Jesus, I declare that Your blood cleanses and heals. It is a priceless gift that saved me from my sins. If it were not for Your shed blood, I would not have my sins forgiven. Your blood washes me and makes me whole. It protects me from the seen and unseen in my life. Thank You for Your blood. I decree and declare the blood of Jesus over my life, my health, my family, my wealth, and the mighty kingdom assignment You have given me to do. All that I accomplish is because of the immeasurable power in Your blood.

മ

CHAPTER 11

CLAIMING VICTORY
OVER THE ENEMY

VICTORY IS YOUR inheritance through Jesus Christ. You're not fighting for victory—you're fighting from it. The enemy is already defeated, but he thrives on deception and distraction. Prayer sharpens your discernment and activates spiritual authority.

When you pray the Word, remind the enemy of his defeat. Declare, "No weapon formed against me shall prosper" and "I trample on every serpent and scorpion through Christ." (See Isaiah 54:17; Luke 10:19.) Victory comes through consistent worship, the Word, and unwavering faith. Even when you feel under attack, stand firm in the truth. Your victory is guaranteed.

> Your right hand, O Lord, has become glorious in power; Your right hand, O Lord, has dashed the enemy in pieces.
> —Exodus 15:6

Lord God, Your right hand has become glorious in power, and it has defeated the enemy. I am so thankful that I do not have to rely on my own wisdom, might, or strength to claim the victory. You have already accomplished that by dashing him to pieces.

**You're not fighting for victory—
you're fighting from it.**

> So David inquired of the Lord, saying, "Shall I pursue this troop? Shall I overtake them?" And He answered him, "Pursue, for you shall surely overtake them and without fail recover all."
> —1 Samuel 30:8

Father, I pray that I inquire as David did in Your Word—that I will be diligent and ask You questions, listen patiently for the Holy Spirit's direction, and then set out to accomplish the task.

You have taken account of my wanderings; put my tears in Your bottle. Are they not recorded in Your book? Then my enemies will turn back in the day when I call; this I know, that God is for me. In God, whose word I praise, in the LORD, whose word I praise, in God have I put my trust and confident reliance; I will not be afraid. What can man do to me?

—PSALM 56:8–11, AMP

Father God, You have taken account of my wanderings and put my tears in Your bottle. Are they not recorded in Your book? Then my enemies will turn back in the day when I call; this I know, that God is for me. In God whose word I praise; in the Lord, whose word I praise; and in God, in whom I have put my trust and confident reliance, I will not be afraid. What can man do to me?

But thanks be to God, who gives us the victory through our Lord Jesus Christ.

—1 CORINTHIANS 15:57

Lord Jesus, I am so grateful. Thanks be to God who gives me the victory through my Lord Jesus Christ.

Now this I say, brethren, that flesh and blood cannot inherit the kingdom of God; nor does corruption inherit incorruption.

—1 CORINTHIANS 15:50

Lord God, I am reminded that neither flesh and blood nor corruption can inherit the kingdom of God.

Though a thousand fall at your side, though ten thousand are dying around you, these evils will not touch you.

—PSALM 91:7, NLT

Abba Father, though there are so many falling and dying around me, their evil ways will not touch me.

What then shall we say to these things? If God is for us, who can be against us?

—ROMANS 8:31

Thank You, Father, that no matter what, as long as You are for me, no one can be against me.

You prepare a feast for me in the presence of my enemies. You honor me by anointing my head with oil. My cup overflows with blessings. Surely your goodness and unfailing love will pursue me all the days of my life, and I will live in the house of the LORD forever.

—PSALM 23:5–6, NLT

Lord, I thank You for setting the table for me in the presence of my enemies. I am grateful for the anointing. The overflow of blessings is in my cup. Goodness and mercy shall follow me forever.

I will establish My covenant between Me and you and your descendants after you throughout their generations for an ever-lasting covenant, to be God to you and to your descendants after you.

—GENESIS 17:7, AMP

Lord, thank You for establishing Your covenant with me and my descendants.

I can do all things through Christ who strengthens me.

—PHILIPPIANS 4:13

Yes, Lord, I can do all things through You who gives me strength.

When this happens, then at last this Scripture will come true—"Death is swallowed up in victory." O death, where then your victory? Where then your sting? For sin—the sting that causes death—will all be gone; and the law, which reveals our sin, will no longer be our judge. How we thank God for all of this! It is he who makes us victorious through Jesus Christ our Lord!

—1 CORINTHIANS 15:54–57, TLB

Almighty God, I thank You that Your Word is true. Death is swallowed up in victory; it has no sting. Sin is gone, and what our sins reveals will not be our judge. I am so glad to know that through Jesus Christ, I have the victory!

But he stationed himself in the middle of that field, defended it, and killed the Philistines. So the LORD brought about a great victory.

—2 SAMUEL 23:12

God, I know You are with me when I stand in the middle of my storm. You defend my cause and destroy the enemy. Thank You, Lord, for bringing me great victory!

He said, "Listen, all you people of Judah and Jerusalem! Listen, King Jehoshaphat! This is what the LORD says: Do not be afraid! Don't be discouraged by this mighty army, for the battle is not yours, but God's."

—2 CHRONICLES 20:15, NLT

Heavenly Father, through Your Word You have always helped others to endure. I shall not be afraid or discouraged, because the battle is not mine but the Lord's.

But He answered and said, "It is written, 'Man shall not live by bread alone, but by every word that proceeds from the mouth of God.'"

—MATTHEW 4:4

Yes, Father, the victory is in Your Word. It is written; I shall live not by bread alone but by every word that comes from the mouth of God.

Simon, stay on your toes. Satan has tried his best to separate all of you from me, like chaff from wheat. Simon, I've prayed for you in particular that you not give in or give out. When you have come through the time of testing, turn to your companions and give them a fresh start.

—LUKE 22:31–32, MSG

Father, I thank You for teaching me to stay on my toes because Satan tries his best to separate me from You. Thank God for covering me so that I will not give in or give out. I will pass this test and give my friends a new start!

I am He who lives, and was dead, and behold, I am alive forevermore. Amen. And I have the keys of Hades and of Death.
—REVELATION 1:18

Lord God, You are He who lives, was dead, and are alive forevermore! You have the keys to hell and death!

&

....

....

....

....

CHAPTER 12

SEEKING DELIVERANCE FROM THE ENEMY

DELIVERANCE IS THE manifestation of God's power to free us from bondage—whether it's sin, fear, generational curses, or demonic oppression. Psalm 34:19 promises, "Many are the afflictions of the righteous, but the LORD delivers him out of them all." Through prayer we declare that Christ's finished work on the cross has broken every chain.

Deliverance begins with repentance, renouncing agreement with lies, and declaring truth. You can declare, "I am free in Jesus' name. Every yoke is destroyed by the anointing."

Don't fear deliverance. It is a gift that restores clarity, peace, and identity. Whether sudden or gradual, deliverance is real and powerful. Keep praying, keep confessing, and keep standing firm in your freedom.

> For I know that this will turn out for my deliverance through your prayer and the supply of the Spirit of Jesus Christ.
> —PHILIPPIANS 1:19

Thank You, Lord, because I know these struggles will result in my deliverance through prayer and the sustaining power of the Spirit of Jesus Christ.

Christ's finished work on the cross has broken every chain.

> And God sent me before you to preserve a posterity [descendants] for you in the earth, and to save your lives by a great deliverance.
> —GENESIS 45:7

Father, I thank You that You have gone before me to prepare the way and to preserve a generational legacy in the earth. You have saved my life by a great deliverance! I am delivered from every setback and setup that tries to distract me from who I am called to be! I walk in freedom, purpose, and divine destiny. I decree that my deliverance is generational—what You've begun in me will bless my children and every generation to come!

O LORD my God, in You I put my trust; save me from all those who persecute me; and deliver me.

—PSALM 7:1

Dear God, in You I put my trust; save me from all those who persecute me and deliver me.

But the LORD your God you shall fear; and He will deliver you from the hand of all your enemies.

—2 KINGS 17:39

Almighty God, I shall fear only You, and You will deliver me from the hand of my enemies.

Everyone who calls upon the name of the Lord will be saved; even in Jerusalem some will escape, just as the Lord has promised, for he has chosen some to survive.

—JOEL 2:32, TLB

Lord, I thank You that all who call on You will be saved. I call on You today and declare that I am saved, delivered, and preserved by Your promise.

And the LORD said to Joshua, "Do not fear them, for I have delivered them into your hand; not a man of them shall stand before you."

—JOSHUA 10:8

Father, I will not be afraid because You have delivered me. I decree and declare that not one person will stand against me.

Then you will emerge from the ambush and take possession of the city, for the LORD your God will hand it over to you.

—JOSHUA 8:7, AMP

Lord God, I thank You that You cause me to rise above every obstacle and every plan set against me. You have given me victory and positioned me to take possession of all that You've promised. Your mighty hand covers me, and by Your power, I will conquer and possess the land You have prepared for me!

And he said: "The LORD is my rock and my fortress and my deliverer."

—2 SAMUEL 22:2

Yes, Lord, You are my rock, my shelter, and my Deliverer.

And the Lord will deliver me from every evil work and preserve me for His heavenly kingdom. To Him be glory forever and ever. Amen!

—2 TIMOTHY 4:18

Jesus, I am grateful that You will deliver me from every evil work and keep me for Your heavenly kingdom. To God be the glory forever!

The LORD is my rock, my fortress, and the One who rescues me; My God, my rock and strength in whom I trust and take refuge; my shield, and the horn of my salvation, my high tower—my stronghold.

—PSALM 18:2, AMP

Father God, You are my rock, my fortress, my rescuer, and my strength in whom I trust. You are my shield, the horn of my salvation, and my stronghold!

He led me to a place of safety; he rescued me because he delights in me.

—PSALM 18:19, NLT

Almighty God, thank You for leading me into a place of safety. You rescue me because You delight in me. I rest secure in Your presence.

So don't be intimidated by them. God, your God, is among you—majestic God, awesome God. God, your God, will get

rid of these nations, bit by bit. You won't be permitted to wipe
them out all at once lest the wild animals take over and over-
whelm you. But God, your God, will move them out of your
way—he'll throw them into a huge panic until there's nothing
left of them. He'll turn their kings over to you and you'll
remove all trace of them under Heaven. Not one person will be
able to stand up to you; you'll put an end to them all.

—DEUTERONOMY 7:23–24, MSG

*Lord, I will not be intimidated by the things in my life that try to
distract me. God, You are majestic and awesome. You will move
them out of my way! You turn kings over and remove all traces of
them. No one will be able to stand up against me because You put
an end to them all.*

&

CHAPTER 13

SPEAKING GOD'S WORD BOLDLY

I MENTIONED IN THE introduction that there is power in the words we speak. What we speak is what we will see. I can take it one step further and say that your words create your reality. When we pray, we are literally speaking the reality we choose to see. You are not just speaking or repeating words; you are releasing divine authority and positioning your life. You see, the enemy rejoices when you say the wrong thing because that becomes your reality.

As long as you keep your mouth closed, as long as you repeat the agenda of hell, you will not see the success that the Lord has for you. But the moment you speak life, the moment you speak the Lord's promises of healing and victory over your situation, alignment takes place. That's why we pray the Scriptures. It is Scripture that allows us to prophesy to our future.

Today, we are not only thinking words; we are speaking the Word. Our declarations are destiny shapers. You and I must keep speaking God's Word until it is in full manifestation in our lives. Power is on display when we speak what God says.

> **As long as you repeat the agenda of hell, you will not see the success that the Lord has for you.**

Now, Lord, look on their threats, and grant to Your servants that with all boldness they may speak Your word.

—Acts 4:29

Father God, I pray for the boldness it takes to speak Your Word. Rebuke those who come against the Word of the Lord that is in my mouth and let it accomplish Your will as You ordain it.

Walk straight, act right, tell the truth.

—Psalm 15:2, MSG

Almighty God, help me walk straight, act right, and tell the truth.

Listen, for I will speak of excellent things, and from the opening of my lips will come right things.

—PROVERBS 8:6

Father, I honor and bless You. I will listen, for I will speak of excellent things. And when I open my lips, I will speak what is right.

A PRAYER TO SPEAK TRUTH WITH POWER

I shall speak the truth with power! Let every evil spirit seeking to attack or derail my calling depart from me, in Jesus' name. Let success and promotion be attached to my life. And in my workplace, let the power of God destroy every enemy of progress, in Jesus' name.

ॐ

CHAPTER 14

THANKING GOD FOR WHAT HE HAS DONE

WHEN MY CHILDREN were young, I taught them early on how to say thank you when they received something. As a father I beamed with pride when I no longer had to remind my children to say those words. Thank you became a permanent fixture in their daily conversation. My daughter will tell you that a simple "thank you" opens my hands just a little wider.

Gratitude is the language of faith. Before you ask God for anything, thank Him for everything. First Thessalonians 5:18 says, "In everything give thanks; for this is the will of God in Christ Jesus for you." Thanksgiving shifts your focus from lack to abundance and from frustration to favor. When you pray with a thankful heart, you acknowledge God's goodness, presence, and power. And like my daughter, you begin to see the blessings of the Lord multiply in your life because the voice of complaining is silenced.

My prayer for you is that you wake up with a heart of gratitude, and as you make it a daily habit to say thank you, heaven will be open over your heart.

> **Gratitude is the language of faith. Before you ask God for anything, thank Him for everything.**

And let the peace that comes from Christ rule in your hearts. For as members of one body you are called to live in peace. And always be thankful.

—COLOSSIANS 3:15, NLT

Almighty God, in a world where peace seems to be obsolete, let the peace that comes from Christ rule my heart. For as members of one body, we are called to live in peace and always be thankful.

Jesus, I thank You for Your love, strength, sacrifice, and presence in my life! You are the ruler of my heart. Although there are times when it seems as if I have forgotten You—not just for what You do but for who You are—You still keep me covered in Your blood! Thank You for keeping me in Your grip and never letting me go, in Jesus' name. Amen!

> **As you make it a daily habit to say thank you, heaven will be open over your heart.**

Amen! Blessing and glory and wisdom, thanksgiving and honor and power and might, be to our God forever and ever. Amen.
—REVELATION 7:12

Yes, God! Blessing, glory, wisdom, thanksgiving, honor, power, and might be to You forever and ever. Amen!

ഇ

....

....

....

....

PART III

BECOME WHO GOD CREATED YOU TO BE

Transformation begins when you allow God to shape your mind, heart, and character. This section will lead you in prayers that help you live fully as the person God designed you to be.

CHAPTER 15

BATTLING FOR A SOUND MIND

IT IS AMAZING how powerful thoughts are. They can construct and shape our lives, and if they are not disciplined, they can be our worst enemy. The devil will attack us with thoughts that try to keep us stagnant and unsure of our future. We must know how to combat these lies and deceptions with the Word.

We read in 2 Timothy 1:7, "God has not given us a spirit of fear, but of power and of love and of a sound mind." In a world that often bombards us with facts and opinions that leave us feeling fearful and confused, we must pray for a mind anchored in the truth. A sound mind is stable, clear, focused, and rooted in Christ. By praying for mental clarity, emotional healing, and spiritual discernment, we are asking God to align our thoughts with the mind of Christ.

If you need God to give you a sound, clear mind, I want you to speak over yourself: "The mind of Christ Jesus lives and operates through me." Don't allow the false narratives and imaginations that come from hell to rule your thoughts; instead, cast them down (2 Cor. 10:5). God can and will calm the storm in your mind, just as easily as Jesus calmed the storm on the sea. As we pray, mental strength will rise, clarity will break forth, and peace will guard our hearts and minds in Christ Jesus.

> **In a world that often bombards us with facts and opinions that leave us feeling fearful and confused, we must pray for a mind anchored in the truth.**

For God did not give us a spirit of timidity (of cowardice, of craven and cringing and fawning fear), but [He has given us a spirit] of power and of love and of calm and well-balanced mind and discipline and self-control.

—2 TIMOTHY 1:7, AMPC

Lord God, You have not given me a spirit of timidity (of cowardice, of craven and cringing and fawning fear) but You have given me a spirit of power and of love and of a calm and well-balanced mind.

And be renewed in the spirit of your mind.

—EPHESIANS 4:23

Father, renew me in the spirit of my mind.

I hope all of you who are mature Christians will see eye-to-eye with me on these things, and if you disagree on some point, I believe that God will make it plain to you.

—PHILIPPIANS 3:15, TLB

Lord God, I thank You that those who are mature in Christ will see eye-to-eye in Your truth. And if I miss it in any way, I trust You to make it plain to me. In Jesus' name, I walk in clarity and understanding by Your Spirit.

> **Don't allow the false narratives and imaginations that come from hell to rule your thoughts; cast them down.**

Those who think they can do it on their own end up obsessed with measuring their own moral muscle but never get around to exercising it in real life. Those who trust God's action in them find that God's Spirit is in them—living and breathing God! Obsession with self in these matters is a dead end; attention to God leads us out into the open, into a spacious, free life. Focusing on the self is the opposite of focusing on God. Anyone completely absorbed in self ignores God, ends up thinking more about self than God. That person ignores who God is and what he is doing. And God isn't pleased at being ignored.

—ROMANS 8:5–8, MSG

Almighty God, I confess that I cannot live this life on my own. Guard my heart from self-reliance and the trap of trusting in my own strength. Keep me from being obsessed with my own moral muscle instead of living out Your truth. I trust Your action within me, knowing that Your Spirit lives and breathes in me. Focusing on my flesh leads only to a dead end, but setting my attention on You leads me into a spacious and free life. Lord, my eyes are fixed on You. I will not ignore You because I do not want You to ignore me. I choose to honor You, walk in step with Your Spirit, and live in the freedom You give.

Then I will raise up for Myself a faithful priest who shall do according to what is in My heart and in My mind. I will build him a sure house, and he shall walk before My anointed forever.

—1 Samuel 2:35

Lord, I bless and honor You, for You have raised me to be a faithful follower of Christ who does what is in Your heart and mind. Thank You for building a stable house for me and empowering me to walk before Your Anointed One forever, bringing glory to Your name.

And Solomon, my son, learn to know the God of your ancestors intimately. Worship and serve him with your whole heart and a willing mind. For the Lord sees every heart and knows every plan and thought. If you seek him, you will find him. But if you forsake him, he will reject you forever.

—1 Chronicles 28:9, nlt

Father God, I choose to know You intimately, to worship, and to serve You with my whole heart and a willing mind. God, You already see every plan and thought in my heart. Because I seek You, I will find You. I will never forsake You, for You are my God forever.

So we built the wall, and the entire wall was joined together up to half its height, for the people had a mind to work.

—Nehemiah 4:6

Lord Jesus, I thank You that I have a mind to work! Strengthen me to build, join together, and raise a higher standard in my life. With Your help I will accomplish all that You have called me to do.

Examine me, O Lord, and try me; test my heart and my mind.

—Psalm 26:2, amp

Abba Father, examine me, prove me, and test my heart and my mind. May the words of my mouth and the meditations of my heart be acceptable in Your sight, O Lord, my strength and my Redeemer (Ps. 19:14).

I, the LORD, search the heart, I test the mind, even to give every man according to his ways, according to the fruit of his doings.
—JEREMIAH 17:10

Lord Jesus, thank You for searching my heart and testing my mind. Let my ways and the fruit of my life be pleasing to You and reward me according to Your righteousness.

This I recall to my mind, therefore I have hope.
—LAMENTATIONS 3:21

Lord Jesus, I recall Your faithfulness to my mind, and therefore I have hope. My thoughts are filled with Your promises, and my hope is secure in You.

For to be carnally minded is death, but to be spiritually minded is life and peace.
—ROMANS 8:6

Almighty God, I refuse to be carnally minded because that leads to death. Instead, I choose to be spiritually minded, which brings life and peace.

And he must be hospitable [to believers, as well as strangers], a lover of what is good, sensible (upright), fair, devout, self-disciplined [above reproach—whether in public or in private].
—TITUS 1:8, AMP

Lord, I choose to be hospitable to both believers and strangers. I love what is good, walk sensibly, live fairly, stay devoted, and practice self-discipline. By Your grace I will live above reproach in public and in private.

That you may with one mind and one mouth glorify the God and Father of our Lord Jesus Christ.
—ROMANS 15:6

*Abba Father—the God and Father of my Lord Jesus Christ—
with one mind my mouth shall glorify You. Let my heart and
words bring You praise.*

Now, friends, read these next words carefully. Slow down and
don't go jumping to conclusions regarding the day when our
Master, Jesus Christ, will come back and we assemble to wel-
come him. Don't let anyone shake you up or get you excited
over some breathless report or rumored letter from me that the
day of the Master's arrival has come and gone. Don't fall for any
line like that.
                              —2 THESSALONIANS 2:1–3, MSG

*Almighty God, I will not be shaken or deceived about the return
of Jesus Christ or any other truth in Your Word. I choose to slow
down, stay watchful, and hold fast to Your truth. I will not fall for
rumors or untruths but remain steady in faith.*

Set your mind on things above, not on things on the earth.
                              —COLOSSIANS 3:2

*In the name of Jesus, today and every day, I shall set my mind on
things above and not on things on the earth.*

Only [be sure to] lead your lives in a manner [that will be]
worthy of the gospel of Christ, so that whether I do come and
see you or remain absent, I will hear about you that you are
standing firm in one spirit [and one purpose], with one mind
striving side by side [as if in combat] for the faith of the gospel.
                              —PHILIPPIANS 1:27, AMP

*Father God, I choose to conduct my life in a way worthy of the
gospel of Christ. I stand firm in a united spirit and purpose,
striving side by side with a single mind for the faith of the gospel.*

Fulfill my joy by being like-minded, having the same love, being
of one accord, of one mind.
                              —PHILIPPIANS 2:2

Lord, I decree and declare that You are fulfilling my joy as I walk with You, having the same love, being in one accord and of one mind.

Have this same attitude in yourselves which was in Christ Jesus [look to Him as your example in selfless humility].

—PHILIPPIANS 2:5, AMP

Father, I choose the attitude of Christ Jesus. I walk in selfless humility, looking to Him as my example.

Let all who are spiritually mature agree on these things. If you disagree on some point, I believe God will make it plain to you.

—PHILIPPIANS 3:15, NLT

Almighty God, help me walk in spiritual maturity in every area of my life. Where I lack understanding, I trust You to make it plain to me.

Don't fret or worry. Instead of worrying, pray. Let petitions and praises shape your worries into prayers, letting God know your concerns. Before you know it, a sense of God's wholeness, everything coming together for good, will come and settle you down. It's wonderful what happens when Christ displaces worry at the center of your life.

—PHILIPPIANS 4:7, MSG

Jesus, I refuse to worry or fret. Instead, I let my petitions and praises shape my worries into prayers. As I tell You everything that concerns me, You will fill me with a sense of wholeness—of everything coming together for good—which will settle me down. Thank You, Jesus, for displacing worry so that You are again the center of my life!

And do not be conformed to this world, but be transformed by the renewing of your mind, that you may prove what is that good and acceptable and perfect will of God.

—ROMANS 12:2

Father, my prayer is that I will not behave like the world but be changed by the renewing of my mind, so that I may establish what is good and acceptable, as well as Your perfect will.

DECLARATION FOR A SOUND MIND

Father, I declare that my mind is made up. It is set on Your Word and Your will for my life. No matter what I see, I will remember and follow Your will. My mind is sold out to Your goodness and faithfulness—not only toward me but also toward my family, friends, and even my enemies. Because my mind is fixed on You, I can declare it is done, and it is so!

∞

CHAPTER 16

CLAIMING THE BENEFITS OF COVENANT WITH GOD

Have you ever accepted a job that didn't come with benefits? If you have, you know how hard it was for you to access certain necessities. One of the many perks of steady employment is the benefits package. It brings the security of knowing certain needs are already covered.

The same is true in the kingdom of God. Psalm 103:2 declares, "Bless the Lord, O my soul, and forget not all His benefits." As children of God, we have access to a "benefits package." He daily loads us with blessings, both seen and unseen (Ps. 68:19).

When we pray, we acknowledge not just who God is but what He has freely given us. These benefits include forgiveness, healing, redemption, love, mercy, provision, and protection. Prayer helps us to remember and rehearse what God has done and what He promises to do.

You don't have to live beneath your inheritance. God's benefits are not earned; they are part of your covenant inheritance through Christ. As you pray from a posture of remembrance and gratitude, your faith will be activated, expectation will rise, and you will step into the fulness of God's promises.

> Blessed be the Lord, who daily loads us with benefits, the God of our salvation!
>
> —Psalm 68:19

Father, You are amazing! Blessed are You, Lord, who gives me benefits daily. You are the God of my salvation.

> He will love you and bless you and multiply you; He will also bless the fruit of your womb and the fruit of your land, your grain and your new wine and your [olive] oil, the offspring of your cattle and the young of your flock, in the land which He swore to your fathers to give you.
>
> —Deuteronomy 7:13, amp

Lord Jesus, I praise and honor You because You love me. You bless me and will multiply me. You will bless the fruit of my womb, the work of my hands, and the fruit of my land. Everything connected to me prospers because of Your covenant promise.

When Job prayed for his friends, the LORD restored his fortunes. In fact, the LORD gave him twice as much as before!

—JOB 42:10, NLT

Father God, I choose to pray for others, just as Job did. I thank You that You are the God who restores and blesses abundantly. I trust You to bring restoration in my life, and I believe You can give me even more than I had before.

Return to the stronghold, you prisoners of hope. Even today I declare that I will restore double to you.

—ZECHARIAH 9:12

Heavenly Father, I return to You, my stronghold. I am a prisoner of hope. Even today, You declare that You will restore double to me.

And all these blessings shall come upon you and overtake you, because you obey the voice of the LORD your God.

—DEUTERONOMY 28:2

Father, I thank You that because of my obedience to You, blessings shall come upon me and overtake me. Your favor pursues me, and I walk in the overflow of Your promises.

For You meet him with blessings of good things; You set a crown of pure gold on his head.

—PSALM 21:3, AMP

Thank You, Father, for meeting me with blessings of good things and placing a crown of pure gold on my head.

May the God of your father help you; may the Almighty bless you with the blessings of the heavens above, and blessings of the watery depths below, and blessings of the breasts and womb.

—GENESIS 49:25, NLT

Lord, I thank You that You are my Helper and my almighty God. You bless me with the riches of heaven above, the abundance of the watery depths below, and the blessings that give and sustain life.

GOD's blessing makes life rich; nothing we do can improve on God.
—PROVERBS 10:22, MSG

Lord, I am grateful because Your blessing makes my life rich. There is nothing I can do to improve on You.

I will make you a great nation; I will bless you and make your name great; and you shall be a blessing.
—GENESIS 12:2

Almighty God, I thank You for making me a great nation, making my name great, blessing me, and empowering me to be a blessing to others.

O my soul, bless GOD. From head to toe, I'll bless his holy name! O my soul, bless GOD, don't forget a single blessing!
—PSALM 103:2, MSG

Father, my soul blesses You. From head to toe, I will bless Your holy name. My soul blesses You and will not forget a single blessing!

But now what can I offer Jehovah for all he has done for me?
—PSALM 116:12, TLB

Dear God, what can I offer You for all You have done for me? My life is my offering. I give myself wholly to You in gratitude and worship.

☙

....

....

....

....

CHAPTER 17

GAINING STRENGTH IN WEAKNESS

I HAVE HEARD OF many people who have been called the strongest person in their circle. It seems they are able to endure trials and tribulations with ease. Maybe you have been labeled as one of those individuals. I want to remind you that even the strongest can grow weary, but God is available to give power to the faint and strength to those who wait on Him (Isa. 40:29–31). God releases strength when we decide to stop striving and start trusting.

By praying for strength, we admit our limitations and invite God's supernatural ability into our weakness. Strength in prayer is not just physical; it is emotional, mental, and spiritual endurance. Even if you are facing a hard season, you can pray that the joy of the Lord will be your strength (Neh. 8:10). Speaking life into weary areas and praying God's Word will recharge your spirit. I want you to receive God's strength as you pray. Keep going, keep believing, and keep standing.

> **God releases strength when we decide to stop striving and start trusting.**

He gives power to the weak, and to those who have no might He increases strength.
—ISAIAH 40:29

Father, I thank You that when I am weak, You give me power. When I have no might, You increase my strength. You are the source of my endurance, the lifter of my head, and the strength of my life. I declare that Your power is made perfect in my weakness, and I rise in the strength of the Lord.

He did not waver at the promise of God through unbelief, but was strengthened in faith, giving glory to God.
—ROMANS 4:20

Thank You, heavenly Father, that I do not waver at Your promises through unbelief. Instead, You strengthen my faith daily. I give You glory, trusting fully that what You have spoken You are faithful to perform.

For You have armed me with strength for the battle; You have subdued under me those who rose up against me.

—PSALM 18:39

Thank You, Lord, for arming me with strength for every battle. You equip me to stand, to fight, and to overcome. I bless You that every enemy who rises against me is subdued beneath me by Your power. Victory belongs to You, and in You I triumph.

It is God who arms me with strength, and makes my way perfect.

—PSALM 18:32

Lord God, You are the One who arms me with strength and makes my way perfect. You prepare my path, steady my steps, and empower me to walk in Your will. I declare that my life is aligned with Your purpose, strengthened by Your hand, and perfected by Your Spirit.

So it shall serve as a sign and a reminder on your [left] hand (arm) and as frontlets between your eyes, for by a strong and powerful hand the LORD brought us out of Egypt.

—EXODUS 13:16, AMP

Father, I honor and bless You for setting reminders before my eyes and upon my hands, keeping me mindful of Your mighty works. It is Your strong hand that has brought me out of Egypt—out of bondage, out of darkness—and into freedom.

The God of my strength, in whom I will trust; my shield and the horn of my salvation, my stronghold and my refuge; my Savior, You save me from violence.

—2 SAMUEL 22:3

Almighty God, You are the God of my strength who I trust. You are my shield and the horn of my salvation. You are my stronghold, my refuge, my Savior, who delivers me from violence and the attack of the enemy. I declare that my life is secure in You.

Let the words of my mouth and the meditation of my heart be acceptable in Your sight, O Lᴏʀᴅ, my strength and my Redeemer.

—Psᴀʟᴍ 19:14

Lord, let the words from my mouth and the meditation of my heart be acceptable in Your sight, O Lord, my strength and my Redeemer.

You have armed me with strength for the battle; you have subdued my enemies under my feet.

—Psᴀʟᴍ 18:39, ɴʟᴛ

God, thank You for arming me with strength for every battle. You have restrained my enemies under my feet.

Don't be impatient. Wait for the Lord, and he will come and save you! Be brave, stouthearted, and courageous. Yes, wait and he will help you.

—Psᴀʟᴍ 27:14, ᴛʟʙ

Jesus, I will not be impatient. I will wait for You, knowing You will come and save me! I will be brave, strong in heart, and courageous. Yes, I will wait so You can help me.

The Lᴏʀᴅ is my strength and my [impenetrable] shield; my heart trusts [with unwavering confidence] in Him, and I am helped; therefore my heart greatly rejoices, and with my song I shall thank Him and praise Him.

—Psᴀʟᴍ 28:7, ᴀᴍᴘ

God, You are my strength and my impenetrable shield. My heart trusts You with unwavering confidence. I know I am being helped, and my heart greatly rejoices. I will sing thanks and praise You.

Wisdom and knowledge will be the stability of your times, and the strength of salvation; the fear of the Lᴏʀᴅ is His treasure.

—Isᴀɪᴀʜ 33:6

Almighty God, I know that wisdom and knowledge will help me stay stable in these times. The strength of Your salvation and my fear of You are Your treasure.

Your Majesty, you are the greatest of kings. The God of heaven has given you sovereignty, power, strength, and honor.

—Daniel 2:37, nlt

God, You are majestic, the greatest of all kings. You are the God of heaven, clothed in sovereignty, power, strength, and honor. None can compare to You, King of kings and Lord of lords.

The Sovereign Lord is my strength! He makes me as sure-footed as a deer, able to tread upon the heights.

—Habakkuk 3:19, nlt

Sovereign Father, You are my strength. You make me surefooted as a deer, steady and able to climb into high places. Thank You for giving me strength to rise and grace to endure.

The Lord says, I will make my people strong with power from me! They will go wherever they wish, and wherever they go they will be under my personal care.

—Zechariah 10:12, tlb

Lord, I thank You for Your promise that You make Your people strong with power from You. I thank You that wherever I go, I am under Your care! My life is secure in Your hands, and You order my steps.

Abraham never wavered in believing God's promise. In fact, his faith grew stronger, and in this he brought glory to God.

—Romans 4:20, nlt

I decree and declare that I will never waver in believing the promise God has for me. Just like Abraham's faith grew stronger, so will mine, and it will bring glory to God.

And He said to me, "My grace is sufficient for you, for My strength is made perfect in weakness." Therefore most gladly

I will rather boast in my infirmities, that the power of Christ may rest upon me.

—2 Corinthians 12:9

Father God, I thank You for Your abundant grace. It is always sufficient for me. When I am weak, Your strength is made perfect in me. I will not hide my weaknesses, for in them the power of Christ rests upon me. I rejoice that Your strength is my covering, and Your power is revealed through my life.

My response is to get down on my knees before the Father, this magnificent Father who parcels out all heaven and earth. I ask him to strengthen you by his Spirit—not a brute strength but a glorious inner strength—that Christ will live in you as you open the door and invite him in. And I ask him that with both feet planted firmly on love, you'll be able to take in with all followers of Jesus the extravagant dimensions of Christ's love. Reach out and experience the breadth! Test its length! Plumb the depths! Rise to the heights! Live full lives, full in the fullness of God.

—Ephesians 3:16–19, msg

Lord, as I pray to You on my knees, I ask You to strengthen me by Your Spirit. I ask that Your Spirit will be inward and that You, Lord, live in me as I open the door and let You in. I let You in so that I may reach out, experience You, test Your length, go deep, rise, and live a full life! In Jesus' name!

I can do all things through Christ who strengthens me.

—Philippians 4:13

Lord, I decree and declare that I can do all things because it is You who gives me strength.

Being strengthened with all power according to his glorious might so that you may have great endurance and patience.

—Colossians 1:11, niv

Abba Father, I shall be strengthened with all power according to Your glorious might so that I may have great endurance and patience.

But may the God of all grace, who called us to His eternal glory by Christ Jesus, after you have suffered a while, perfect, establish, strengthen, and settle you.

—1 PETER 5:10

Dear God, I know the enemy is trying to intimidate and discourage me, but the work You've called me to will not stop. I will continue with greater determination. I know You will use the hardships and challenges to perfect, establish, strengthen, and settle me.

Your strength is all I need. With every battle it's Your strength that keeps me. In every moment of weakness, it's Your strength that empowers me. And as I approach every clear and perfect path, it is Your strength that pushes me to walk through it.

&

CHAPTER 18

LIVING IN RIGHTEOUSNESS

RIGHTEOUSNESS IS NOT something that is earned; it is a gift received through faith in Jesus Christ. Second Corinthians 5:21 declares, "He made Him who knew no sin to be sin for us, that we might become the righteousness of God in Him." This gift transforms our prayer life. You see, despite what we have done in the past, as believers in Christ, we have been extended a gift that makes us worthy to pray. When you pray from that place of righteousness, you pray with boldness and confidence, knowing you are no longer condemned—you are covered. It is Christ's righteousness that enables us to reflect His holiness.

As we live and pray from this position, we begin to see our lives and decisions reflect the protection of righteousness. His righteousness becomes our protection and sustains our identity in Christ. Remember, the righteousness of God has been given to every believer. Through Christ we have full access to God, and we cannot be denied. We can go boldly before His throne of grace. It is our responsibility to walk daily in righteousness, allowing it to shape every decision we make.

> **Righteousness is not something that is earned;
> it is a gift received through faith in Jesus.**

Stand therefore, having girded your waist with truth, having put on the breastplate of righteousness.
—EPHESIANS 6:14

Father, I pray and stand, therefore, having girded my waist with truth and having put on the breastplate of righteousness. I declare and decree that I shall live a life of righteousness! No matter the battle, the victory, or the struggle, it is all in Your divine will so Your righteousness in me will be seen. I decree and declare that my mind is right, my actions are right, and my thought processes are right before You. I pray that everyone I come in contact with will say I am a changed person, and my response will be right! In the name of Jesus, help me stay right.

For it is by believing in your heart that *you are made right* with God, and it is by openly declaring your faith that you are saved.

—Romans 10:10, nlt, emphasis added

Lord God, it is by believing in my heart that I am made right with God, and it is by openly declaring to my Father that I am saved.

He shall receive blessing from the Lord, and righteousness from the God of his salvation.

—Psalm 24:5

Mighty God, I pray I shall receive a blessing from the Lord and righteousness from the God of my salvation.

Whoever pursues righteousness and unfailing love will find life, righteousness, and honor.

—Proverbs 21:21, nlt

Dear God, when I pursue righteous and Your never-failing love, I will find life, righteousness, and honor.

But now God has shown us a different way to heaven—not by "being good enough" and trying to keep his laws, but by a new way (though not new, really, for the Scriptures told about it long ago). Now God says he will accept and acquit us—declare us "not guilty"—if we trust Jesus Christ to take away our sins. And we all can be saved in this same way, by coming to Christ, no matter who we are or what we have been like.

—Romans 3:22, tlb

Heavenly Father, I rejoice that I am accepted in You and declared not guilty—not by my works but by faith in Him who took away my sins. No matter who I was or what I have done, I can come to Christ just as I am. No matter what people may say or think, in Him I am saved, I am free, and I am made new.

How? you ask. In Christ. God put the wrong on him who never did anything wrong, so we could be put right with God.
—2 Corinthians 5:21, msg

Thank You, Father, for giving Your Son, Jesus, as the sacrifice for my sin. He who knew no wrong became sin for me so that I might be made right with You. I thank You that through His righteousness, I now stand forgiven and accepted in Your sight.

I walk in righteousness, in paths of justice.
—Proverbs 8:20, nlt

I decree and declare that I walk in righteousness and in the path of what is right.

He shall pray to God, and He will delight in him, He shall see His face with joy, for He restores to man His righteousness.
—Job 33:26

Father, when I pray to You, I will find delight in You. I shall see Your face with joy, and You will restore to me Your righteousness.

I will praise the Lord according to His righteousness, and will sing praise to the name of the Lord Most High.
—Psalm 7:17

Father, I will praise You according to Your righteousness. I will sing praise to You, Lord Most High.

ॐ

CHAPTER 19

TRUSTING GOD FULLY

Every time I get in my car, I trust that my GPS, or navigation system, will get me to my destination without any issues. I trust it to show me the fastest route to my destination with little to no traffic. So why do we sometimes put more trust in computer software and apps than we do in the One who causes us to breathe? Trust is the foundation of genuine faith. Proverbs 3:5–6, tells us, "Trust in the Lord with all your heart, and lean not on your own understanding."

> **God develops our trust in Him
> as we follow His lead.**

When we pray, we surrender control and place our confidence in God's wisdom, timing, and plan. Much like a GPS, the Father leads us down the right path, and if something happens along the way, whether good or bad, His hand guides us to the next place. In the end we will still reach our destination. When we trust God, we're saying, "Even when I can't trace You, I will still trust You."

The prayers in this chapter speak to how we can trust God when we cannot see Him at work in our lives and when we don't hear His voice as loudly as before. Whether we think we know where He is leading us, we should always take a posture of obedience. God develops our trust in Him as we follow His lead. Even when we can't trace Him, we can have confidence that He will never fail us.

Trust in the Lord with all your heart, and lean not on your own understanding; in all your ways acknowledge Him, and He shall direct your paths.

—Proverbs 3:5–6

Lord God, I will trust You with all my heart and lean not on my own understanding. In all my ways, I will acknowledge You, and You shall direct my paths.

As for God, His way is perfect; the word of the LORD is proven; He is a shield to all who trust in Him.

—2 SAMUEL 22:31

Father, I will follow You. Your way is perfect, Your Word is proven, and You are a shield to all who trust in You.

With a view to this we toil and strive, [yes and] suffer reproach, because we have [fixed our] hope on the living God, Who is the Savior (Preserver, Maintainer, Deliverer) of all men, especially of those who believe (trust in, rely on, and adhere to Him).

—1 TIMOTHY 4:10, AMPC

Lord, I strive, work, and fix my hope on You, the living God. You are the Savior, Preserver, Maintainer, and Deliverer of everyone who trusts in You. I believe Your Word is true, and I, too, trust and rely on You.

Though He slay me, yet will I trust Him. Even so, I will defend my own ways before Him.

—JOB 13:15

Amid my trial, Lord, though You slay me, yet will I trust You.

In Him you also trusted, after you heard the word of truth, the gospel of your salvation; in whom also, having believed, you were sealed with the Holy Spirit of promise.

—EPHESIANS 1:13

Heavenly Father, I trust Your Word. Having believed, I have been sealed with the promise of the Holy Spirit.

God blesses those who obey him; happy the man who puts his trust in the LORD.

—PROVERBS 16:20, TLB

Lord, thank You for blessing me because of my obedience to You. I am happy because I trust You!

Every word of God is tried and purified; He is a shield to those who trust and take refuge in Him.

—PROVERBS 30:5, AMPC

Almighty God, I have tried Your Word, and it is a shield for me. I trust and stay protected in You.

Blessed is the man who trusts in the LORD, and whose hope is the LORD.

—JEREMIAH 17:7

Father, I know my life is blessed because I trust and put my hope in You!

A DECLARATION OF TRUST

Father, I take a stand in the name of Jesus and decree and declare that I trust You! The enemy tries to make me doubt, but I trust You! The enemy tries to bring distractions, but I trust You! The enemy tries to distract me with lies and deception, but I trust You! The enemy tries to make me second-guess and sometimes even quit believing, wanting me to abort what You already ordained, but I trust You! Yes, God, I trust You!

&

CHAPTER 20

REMAINING FAITHFUL

ONE OF THE many characteristics of God is His faithfulness. Because He is faithful, He calls us to the same character. If we are in Christ, we should reflect His attributes. Many of us, however, are more faithful to our jobs and to our problems than we are to the things of God. We need to decide today to keep the agreement we made with heaven when we accepted Christ as Lord and Savior.

We serve a consistent God, who is faithful in His love toward us, keeping His promises, and His nature. As we pray, we are asking Him to continuously empower us to be committed, but what does that look like? Among other things, it is through purpose, earthly relationships, and our devotion to Him that we demonstrate our faithfulness. We must remain steady even when it is hard, because our faithfulness will lead to fruitfulness in the souls we win for Christ, the spiritual battles we win in His name, and the glory He receives because of our consistency. We can do it!

> Through the LORD's mercies we are not consumed, because His compassions fail not. They are new every morning; great is Your faithfulness.
> —LAMENTATIONS 3:22–23

Lord God, Your steadfast love never ceases, and Your mercies never come to an end. They are new every morning. Great is Your faithfulness!

> Your faithfulness endures to all generations; You established the earth, and it abides.
> —PSALM 119:90

Almighty God, Your faithfulness endures to all generations. You established the earth, and it abides.

Trust in the Lord instead. Be kind and good to others; then you will live safely here in the land and prosper, feeding in safety.

—Psalm 37:3, tlb

Father, I trust in You. I choose to be kind and good to others. Because I trust and obey, I will live in safety, prosper, and be fed securely by Your hand.

May the Lord repay every man for his righteousness and his faithfulness; for the Lord delivered you into my hand today, but I would not stretch out my hand against the Lord's anointed.

—1 Samuel 26:23

Our faithfulness will lead to fruitfulness.

Thank You, God, for being the One who repays us in righteousness and faithfulness. I am grateful that You delivered me. Nothing will be against me because I am Your anointed vessel.

I will betroth you to Me in faithfulness, and you shall know the Lord.

—Hosea 2:20

Lord, I thank You that You have betrothed me to Yourself in faithfulness. I will remain connected to You and grow in knowing You more and more.

Your faithfulness is from generation to generation; You have established the earth, and it stands fast.

—Psalm 119:90, ampc

Lord Jesus, You are faithful from generation to generation. You established the earth, and it stands firm by Your Word. I trust in Your unshakable faithfulness in my life.

O Lord, I will honor and praise your name, for you are my God; you do such wonderful things! You planned them long ago, and now you have accomplished them, just as you said!

—Isaiah 25:1, tlb

I honor and praise You, Lord. Thank You for the wonderful things that You planned for my life long ago. You have accomplished them just as You said, and You will continue to perform Your Word.

A DECLARATION OF GOD'S FAITHFULNESS

God, You are faithful! Your faithfulness lets me know I don't need to count on anyone but You! You are a covenant-keeping God!

❧

....

....

....

....

CHAPTER 21

ENDURING HARD TRIALS

Endurance is the ability to keep going when everything in you wants to give up. Endurance is the spiritual stamina that carries you through trials, delays, and long seasons of testing. James 1:12 (NIV) says, "Blessed is the one who perseveres under trial because, having stood the test, that person will receive the crown of life that the Lord has promised to those who love him." Prayer strengthens our endurance by anchoring us in God's promises when circumstances try to wear us down. When you feel weary, remember God is not only with you; He is strengthening you.

Endurance doesn't mean you won't feel tired or frustrated, because you will. It means you press on anyway, trusting that God is working behind the scenes. We must be settled in our spirit that our trust in the Lord, while we are waiting, becomes perseverance, as we walk by faith, not by sight.

As you pray, God will bless you with strength, renewed focus, and the patience to continue running. Progress may appear slow or even invisible, but your spiritual muscles are being built, allowing you to stand the test of time. You are being refined for greater, and your reward is waiting for you on the other side.

> **God is not only with you; He is strengthening you.**

When you feel like giving up, use these scriptures to pray God's Word over your life.

> For you have need of endurance, so that after you have done the will of God, you may receive the promise.
> —HEBREWS 10:36

Father God, I have need of endurance. Help me realize my need so that after I have done the will of God, I may receive the promise.

Looking unto Jesus, the author and finisher of our faith, who for the joy that was set before Him endured the cross, despising the shame, and has sat down at the right hand of the throne of God.
—HEBREWS 12:2

God Almighty, I look to You, the author and finisher of my faith. You endured the cross with joy, despising its shame—all for me. Now You are at the right hand of the throne of God.

Therefore we also, since we are surrounded by so great a cloud of witnesses, let us lay aside every weight, and the sin which so easily ensnares us, and let us run with endurance the race that is set before us.
—HEBREWS 12:1

Father, I lay aside every weight and the sin which so easily ensnares us, and I will run with endurance the race set before me.

I press on toward the goal to win the prize for which God has called me heavenward in Christ Jesus.
—PHILIPPIANS 3:14, NIV

Lord God Almighty, strengthen me to press on toward the goal to win the prize for which You have called me heavenward in Christ Jesus.

Endure suffering along with me, as a good soldier of Christ Jesus.
—2 TIMOTHY 2:3, NLT

Yes, Lord, I will endure suffering along with You, as a good soldier of Christ Jesus.

Oh, give thanks to the LORD, for He is good! For His mercy endures forever.
—PSALM 118:29

Father, I give You thanks because You are good, and Your mercy endures forever.

The LORD will work out his plans for my life—for your faithful love, O LORD, endures forever. Don't abandon me, for you made me.

—PSALM 138:8, NLT

Lord, I know You will work out Your plans for my life. You are faithful, and Your love for me endures forever. With Your strength, I can, I shall, and I will endure!

&

CHAPTER 22

WAITING PATIENTLY ON THE LORD

W HEN I WAS growing up, the older generation used to say, "Don't pray for patience because you'll be tested in that very thing." There was some truth to that, but might I add, patience is one of the most powerful forms of trust that we can exhibit to our heavenly Father. We know that patience is a fruit of the Spirit, and it is one of the promises the Lord released to us. One of the struggles we have in this world is that so many things can come instantly.

I never thought I would see the day when you can even bake a cake in a microwave. But that is the day in which we live. Beloved, when we have patience, we allow God to perfect His work in us. Patience is simply the grace to wait. It gives us the strength to not complain or give up. We are allowing the Lord to teach us how to wait well so we are strengthened. I want to warn you that though we practice patience, we do not sit and do nothing. We are exercising our full trust in God, while doing what is right, knowing He is faithful to complete His promises.

The weight in waiting reminds me that Jesus, the One who is carrying it all, is still in control!

Knowing that the testing of your faith produces patience.
—JAMES 1:3

Lord Jesus, I thank You for knowing that the testing of my faith produces patience.

So it is good to wait quietly for salvation from the LORD.
—LAMENTATIONS 3:26, NLT

Father, thank You for teaching me that it is good to wait quietly for salvation from You.

But let patience have its perfect work, that you may be perfect and complete, lacking nothing.
—JAMES 1:4

Abba Father, help me let patience have its perfect work so that I may be perfect and complete, lacking nothing.

But those who wait on the LORD shall renew their strength; they shall mount up with wings like eagles, they shall run and not be weary, they shall walk and not faint.

—ISAIAH 40:31

Almighty God, I thank You that as I wait upon You, my strength is renewed. I will mount up with wings like eagles. I will run and not grow weary. I will walk and not faint, for Your power sustains me. My hope is in You, and in You I will not be shaken.

Wait on the LORD; be of good courage, and He shall strengthen your heart; Wait, I say, on the LORD!

—PSALM 27:14

Father, I will wait on You. While I wait, I shall have good courage, knowing You will strengthen my heart. Yes, I shall wait on You!

The LORD is good to those who wait for Him, to the soul who seeks Him.

—LAMENTATIONS 3:25

Thank You, Father, for being so good to me because I wait on You, and my soul seeks You.

Now may the LORD direct your hearts into the love of God and into the patience of Christ.

—2 THESSALONIANS 3:5

Almighty God, direct my heart into Your love and into having the patience of Christ.

And the seeds that fell on the good soil represent honest, good-hearted people who hear God's word, cling to it, and patiently produce a huge harvest.

—LUKE 8:15, NLT

Father God, I ask You to make my heart good soil—honest, pure, and open before You. Let me be one who hears Your Word, clings to it, and refuses to let it go. By Your Spirit help me endure with patience so that my life produces a great and lasting harvest for Your glory.

Consider it nothing but joy, my brothers and sisters, whenever you fall into various trials. Be assured that the testing of your faith [through experience] produces endurance [leading to spiritual maturity, and inner peace]. And let endurance have its perfect result and do a thorough work, so that you may be perfect and completely developed [in your faith], lacking in nothing.
—JAMES 1:2–4, AMP

Lord God, I choose to count every trial as joy, knowing that the testing of my faith produces endurance. Thank You that through these tests You are shaping me, helping me become spiritually mature and giving me peace. Father, let endurance complete its perfect result and thorough work in me so that I may be whole, completely developed in my faith, and lacking nothing.

Remembering without ceasing your work of faith, labor of love, and patience of hope in our Lord Jesus Christ in the sight of our God and Father.
—1 THESSALONIANS 1:3

Yes, God, I remember the work of faith, labor of love, and patience of hope in You, my Father and my God.

෯

....

....

....

....

CHAPTER 23

BECOMING A NEW YOU

IN CHRIST YOU are not a better version of yourself; you have a brand-new nature. Second Corinthians 5:17 (KJV) says, "Therefore if any man be in Christ, he is a new creature: old things are passed away; behold, all things are become new." When you pray about becoming new, you're embracing spiritual transformation over behavior modification. As believers we should pray that the Lord would renew our mind while reshaping our desires so that our lives become aligned with His will. The new you will walk in purpose, power, and purity. So don't let the past define you as if your old nature were still alive. Let the Word define your future. You've been redeemed, restored, and reset for greatness!

> Therefore, if anyone is in Christ, he is a new creation; old things have passed away; behold, all things have become new.
> —2 CORINTHIANS 5:17

> *It is not new clothes or new money that make me new. Your Word says that I am new, and I declare it is so!*

> Behold, I will do a new thing, now it shall spring forth; shall you not know it? I will even make a road in the wilderness and rivers in the desert.
> —ISAIAH 43:19

> *Almighty God, You will do a new thing. Now it shall spring forth. Shall I not know it? You will even make a road in the wilderness and rivers in the desert.*

> And have put on the new man who is renewed in knowledge according to the image of Him who created him.
> —COLOSSIANS 3:10

Father, I honor You and have put on the new man, who is renewed in knowledge according to the image of the One who created me.

Great is his faithfulness; his mercies begin afresh each morning.
—LAMENTATIONS 3:23, NLT

Lord, thank You for being so faithful and giving me new, fresh mercies every morning.

I will give you a new heart and put a new spirit within you; I will take the heart of stone out of your flesh and give you a heart of flesh.
—EZEKIEL 36:26

Thank You, Jesus, for giving me a new heart and spirit. And thank You for taking out the stony heart and replacing it with a heart of flesh.

> **Don't let the past define you as if your old nature were still alive. Let the Word define your future.**

So now I am giving you a new commandment: Love each other. Just as I have loved you, you should love each other.
—JOHN 13:34, NLT

Lord God, I will keep Your commandment to love everyone. I am able to love others because You first loved me.

And put on the new nature (the regenerate self) created in God's image, [Godlike] in true righteousness and holiness.
—EPHESIANS 4:24, AMPC

Father, I start my change by putting on a new nature. I was created in Your image, in true righteousness and holiness. And here I will remain.

I will praise You, for I am fearfully and wonderfully made; marvelous are Your works, and that my soul knows very well.
—PSALM 139:14

Almighty God, I praise You because I am fearfully and wonderfully made! All You do is marvelous. My souls knows this well.

Don't lie to one another. You're done with that old life. It's like a filthy set of ill-fitting clothes you've stripped off and put in the fire. Now you're dressed in a new wardrobe. Every item of your new way of life is custom-made by the Creator, with his label on it. All the old fashions are now obsolete. Words like Jewish and non-Jewish, religious and irreligious, insider and outsider, uncivilized and uncouth, slave and free, mean nothing. From now on everyone is defined by Christ, everyone is included in Christ.
—COLOSSIANS 3:10–11, MSG

Yes, Lord, I bless You and will not lie. I am done with the old life I was living. Those old, filthy clothes are gone! I have a new wardrobe, and it has been custom-made by the Creator Himself! What was old on me is no more. I am no longer a slave! I am free and defined by God's Word.

Again, a new commandment I write to you, which thing is true in Him and in you, because the darkness is passing away, and the true light is already shining.
—1 JOHN 2:8

Father, I am blessed as I remind myself of Your new commandment in Christ. I rejoice knowing that the darkness is passing away and that Your light is already shining within me. Thank You for letting me walk in that light and experience Your truth, love, and guidance each day.

PART IV

BECOME WHOLE
IN CHRIST

God's desire is to heal every area of your
life: spirit, soul, and body. This section
will guide you in prayers for freedom,
restoration, and renewal so you can live
in the wholeness Christ provides.

CHAPTER 24

OVERCOMING ADDICTION

ADDICTION IS MORE than a physical battle; it's spiritual. You need more than willpower to overcome it. You need God's power. Unfortunately, we live in a time when almost everyone is either dealing with an addiction or knows someone who is. Yet there is hope. Freedom from addictive behaviors is possible for those who truly desire to be free.

Galatians 5:1 (NIV) declares, "It is for freedom that Christ has set us free." When praying to overcome addiction, we must remember that it is— and will always be—Jesus who destroys the yokes and burdens that try to overcome us (Isa. 10:27). It does not matter whether the addiction is to food, illegal substances, the approval of others, or negative patterns and mindsets. Deliverance comes through the blood of Jesus.

If someone is battling addiction, in addition to praying against it, they must also surrender their will and ways to the Lord. And they must be ready for the warfare that is tied to the addiction. It was warfare—in the form of trauma, bad habits, and ungodly desires—that led to addiction, and it will be warfare in the spirit that brings freedom.

> **It is Jesus who destroys the yokes and burdens that try to overcome us.**

If you've been battling addiction of any kind, I want you to declare: "I am not a slave to *anything* but righteousness. The grip of addiction is broken over my life and everyone I love!" Be consistent in this declaration and allow others to hold you accountable as you embrace God's grace and freedom. Whoever the Son sets free is free indeed (John 8:36).

No temptation has overtaken you that is not common to man.
God is faithful, and he will not let you be tempted beyond your
ability, but with the temptation he will also provide the way of
escape, that you may be able to endure it.
—1 CORINTHIANS 10:13, ESV

Father, I thank You for being faithful and that with every temptation You have already planned an escape for me. I thank You that these temptations are no different than what others are experiencing and that You are showing me a way out.

Do not get drunk on wine, which leads to debauchery. Instead, be filled with the Spirit.

—EPHESIANS 5:18, NIV

Father, I thank You that I will not be drunk with wine or enslaved to any substance, but I will be filled with Your Spirit. Addiction has no place in my life or in my bloodline. I walk in wisdom and in the power of Your Spirit. Amen.

For I know that good itself does not dwell in me, that is, in my sinful nature. For I have the desire to do what is good, but I cannot carry it out.

—ROMANS 7:18

Father, I know that nothing good dwells in my sinful nature. I cannot do good in my own strength, but I know that with Your help I can overcome the desires of my flesh. Fill me with Your Spirit so I can walk in Your will.

Therefore, I urge you, brothers and sisters, in view of God's mercy, to offer your bodies as a living sacrifice, holy and pleasing to God—this is your true and proper worship. Do not conform to the pattern of this world, but be transformed by the renewing of your mind. Then you will be able to test and approve what God's will is—his good, pleasing and perfect will.

—ROMANS 12:1–2, NIV

Father, I present my body as a living sacrifice, holy and pleasing to You, which is my true and proper worship. I will not conform to the pattern of this world but be transformed by the renewing of my mind. Keep me from being consumed by my flesh's desires. May my life reflect Your good, pleasing, and perfect will.

If we confess our sins, he is faithful and just to forgive us our sins and to cleanse us from all unrighteousness.

—1 JOHN 1:9, ESV

Father, I confess the sin of addiction and declare that I am for-given, I am free, and I will walk in the righteousness of God.

Be sober-minded; be watchful. Your adversary the devil prowls around like a roaring lion, seeking someone to devour.

—1 Peter 5:8, esv

Lord, thank You for making me sober-minded. I know the enemy comes to cloud my judgment and make me succumb to addiction, but I will not allow my flesh to be devoured by sin. Thank You for helping me to be watchful in what I do.

So if the son sets you free, you will be free indeed.

—John 8:36, niv

Lord, I thank You that I am free from the bondage of addiction. You have made me free, and free I will remain. I will not allow my flesh to be bound by that addiction ever again.

"But I will restore you to health and heal your wounds," declares the Lord, "because you are called an outcast, Zion for whom no one cares."

—Jeremiah 30:17, niv

Lord, thank You for restoring my mind, spirit, and body to a healthy place in You. Thank You for healing me from old wounds that caused me to turn to addiction. I declare that I am restored so that I may be effective in my work for You.

Like a city whose walls are broken through is a person who lacks self-control.

—Proverbs 25:28, niv

Lord, I thank You that I walk in self-control. My life is not like a broken city without walls. The enemy cannot infiltrate me, for I am disciplined and free from the pull of addiction.

For the grace of God has appeared that offers salvation to all people.

—Titus 2:11–12, niv

Lord, I receive Your grace that brings salvation. Your grace is sufficient for me, teaching me to say no to ungodliness. I walk in freedom, wholeness, and victory over addiction.

Blessed is the one who perseveres under trial because, having stood the test, that person will receive the crown of life that the Lord has promised to those who love him. When tempted, no one should say, "God is tempting me." For God cannot be tempted by evil, nor does he tempt anyone; but each person is tempted when they are dragged away by their own evil desire and enticed. Then, after desire has conceived, it gives birth to sin; and sin, when it is full-grown, gives birth to death.

—JAMES 1:12–15, NIV

Lord, I thank You that when I persevere under trial, I receive the crown of life You have promised. I refuse the lies that make temptation or addiction seem natural or acceptable. I stand firm and say no to the temptation. As I do, You have a crown of life waiting for me. This is my promise because You love me.

Dear friends, I urge you, as foreigners and exiles, to abstain from sinful desires, which wage war against your soul.

—1 PETER 2:11, NIV

Lord, I thank You that I have the self-control to not give in to fleshly desires and sin against my body. I will not let my flesh win. Instead, I accept You as my help in this war with my flesh and the enemy.

And lead us not into temptation, but deliver us from the evil one.

—MATTHEW 6:13, NIV

Lord, I will not be tempted by addiction because You have delivered me. I thank You that it is so!

I can do all this through him who gives me strength.

—PHILIPPIANS 4:13, NIV

Lord, thank You for giving me strength and courage to know that I can overcome addiction because of You. I surrender my flesh to You, knowing that You are helping me obtain the victory.

⋈

CHAPTER 25

BECOMING WHOLE AGAIN

WHENEVER JESUS PERFORMED miracles, He didn't just heal one part of the person. He would often command the person to "be made whole" (John 5:6, KJV). To be whole means nothing is missing or broken, and the spirit, soul, and body are in alignment with God's design. When Jesus enters our lives, He deals with the totality of who we are in the spirit so we can experience the benefits of freedom in the natural realm.

In Luke 17:19 (KJV), Jesus told a man He healed, "Thy faith hath made thee whole." Wholeness is more than physical healing; it includes emotional stability, mental peace, spiritual clarity, and much more. When we pray for wholeness, the Lord mends the parts of our lives that have been fractured by trauma, sin, storms, and other issues, and He restores us from the inside out.

You are a kingdom heir, and being whole is your inheritance in the covenant of God. The Father wants you well, balanced, and walking in the fullness of Christ. If you need to be made whole, pray the following scriptures and receive freedom by faith:

> Then I will give them a heart to know Me, that I am the LORD; and they shall be My people, and I will be their God, for they shall return to Me with their whole heart.
>
> —JEREMIAH 24:7

Father, I declare that Jesus has made me whole in every area of my life, and there I will remain! Lord God, give me a heart to know You. You are the Lord, and I am Your child, for I turn to You with my whole heart.

Now may the God of peace Himself sanctify you through and through [that is, separate you from profane and vulgar things, make you pure and whole and undamaged—consecrated to Him—set apart for His purpose]; and may your spirit and soul and body be kept complete and [be found] blameless at the coming of our Lord Jesus Christ.

—1 THESSALONIANS 5:23, AMP

I pray that the God of peace Himself will sanctify me through and through—that You will separate me from profane and vulgar things, make me pure and whole, keep me undamaged, and conse-crate me and set me apart for Your purpose. Lord, may my spirit, soul, and body be kept complete. May I be found blameless at the coming of my Lord Jesus Christ.

If then your whole body is full of light, having no part dark, the whole body will be full of light, as when the bright shining of a lamp gives you light.

—LUKE 11:36

Father God, I pray that my whole body will be full of light, having no part dark. May my life be full of light, like a bright shining lamp giving light.

For length of days and years of life [worth living], and tran-quility and prosperity [the wholeness of life's blessings] they will add to you.

—PROVERBS 3:2, AMP

Lord God, add to me length of days and years of life worth living, along with tranquility and prosperity—the wholeness of life's blessings.

છ

CHAPTER 26

BELIEVING FOR HEALING

WHEN I PLAYED football as a young person, it was not uncommon for me to get injured in some form or fashion. The pain would be excruciating at times, and I would run to my mother for prayer. Eventually, the pain would fade, and I would go back to playing, as though nothing had ever happened. As I grew older, I realized that healing wasn't just for physical ailments; it's for emotional wounds too. I found that I was in need of healing from past broken relationships. Others may need healing from spiritual brokenness. Let's not put limits on God. He wants to bring healing in all areas of our lives.

The Bible promises that "by His stripes we are healed" (Isa. 53:5). When we pray for healing, we stand on the authority of God's Word and Jesus' finished work on the cross. Whether the healing process is immediate or progressive, God is Jehovah Rapha, the Lord who heals.

The scriptures in this chapter will lead you to receive healing in all areas of your life. I speak over your life that as you pray, you will see God restore your heart and give you peace in your mind. Your body and home will be made whole. You will not be discouraged by your symptoms; instead, you will trust that God still heals today. Declare by faith, "Yes, I am healed! By the stripes and the touch of Jesus, I am healed!"

Heal me, O LORD, and I shall be healed; save me, and I shall be saved, for You are my praise.

—JEREMIAH 17:14

Lord, You are my Savior and Healer. I pray as Your Word declares: Heal me, and I shall be healed; save me, and I shall be saved, for You are my praise. I worship You alone.

But He was wounded for our transgressions, He was bruised for our iniquities; the chastisement for our peace was upon Him, and by His stripes we are healed.

—ISAIAH 53:5

Jesus, I honor and bless You. You were wounded for my transgressions, and You were bruised for my iniquities. The chastisement for my peace was upon You. And by Your stripes I am healed.

I am not even worthy to come and meet you. Just say the word from where you are, and my servant will be healed.

—Luke 7:7, nlt

Father, I trust fully in Your authority and power. Just speak the word, and healing will be released. I believe that at Your word, sickness must go, and I will be made whole.

Behold, I will bring it health and cure, and I will cure them, and will reveal unto them the abundance of peace and truth.

—Jeremiah 33:6, kjv

Thank You, Lord, for bringing health to me, curing me, and now revealing to me an abundance of peace and truth.

> **When we pray for healing, we stand on the authority of God's Word and Jesus' finished work on the cross.**

And when he had called unto him his twelve disciples, he gave them power against unclean spirits, to cast them out, and to heal all manner of sickness and all manner of disease.

—Matthew 10:1, kjv

You also have given me power against all unclean spirits—to cast them out and to heal all manner of sickness and all diseases.

But for you who fear my name, the Sun of Righteousness will rise with healing in his wings. And you will go free, leaping with joy like calves let out to pasture.

—Malachi 4:2, tlb

Thank You, Jesus. You have already risen with healing in Your wings, and I am free, leaping with joy like a calf let out to pasture.

But he was wounded and bruised for our sins. He was beaten
that we might have peace; he was lashed—and we were
healed!

—ISAIAH 53:5, TLB

Jesus, You were wounded and bruised for my sins; You were
beaten, so now I can have peace, and because You were lashed, I
am now healed.

He personally carried the load of our sins in his own body when
he died on the cross so that we can be finished with sin and live
a good life from now on. For his wounds have healed ours!

—1 PETER 2:24, TLB

Praise the LORD, my soul, and forget not all his benefits—who
forgives all your sins and heals all your diseases.

—PSALM 103:2–3, NIV

I bless You with all my soul, Lord, for You said not to forget Your
benefits. Thank You for forgiving all my sins and healing all my
diseases.

And if the Spirit of him who raised Jesus from the dead is living
in you, he who raised Christ from the dead will also give life to
your mortal bodies because of his Spirit who lives in you.

—ROMANS 8:11, NIV

I thank You, Lord Jesus, that the Holy Spirit, who raised You
from the dead, is living in me and has given life to my mortal body.

He sent his word, and healed them, and delivered them from
their destructions.

—PSALM 107:20, KJV

I rejoice, for Your Word has healed me and delivered me from
destruction.

The right hand of the LORD is exalted: the right hand of the
LORD doeth valiantly. I shall not die, but live, and declare the
works of the LORD.

—PSALM 118:16–17, KJV

By Your right hand, Lord, You do great things. For I shall not die but live to declare Your wonderful works.

That it might be fulfilled which was spoken by Isaiah the prophet, saying: "He Himself took our infirmities and bore our sicknesses."
—Matthew 8:17

You took my infirmities, so I don't have them. You carried away my diseases, so they are far from me. I know that Your life is now flowing through me, and You have brought healing to every cell of my being.

No evil shall befall you, nor shall any plague come near your dwelling.
—Psalm 91:10

Thank You, Lord, for keeping evil and plagues away from me and my home.

Make this your common practice: Confess your sins to each other and pray for each other so that you can live together whole and healed.
—James 5:16, msg

I join with other believers in confessing our sins to and praying for one another so that we can live together whole and healed.

Listen, son of mine, to what I say. Listen carefully. Keep these thoughts ever in mind; let them penetrate deep within your heart, for they will mean real life for you and radiant health.
—Proverbs 4:20–22, tlb

I listen to Your words carefully. I keep them always in mind so they can penetrate deeply into my heart—for they mean real life to me and health to all my flesh.

God will accept all people in every nation who trust God as Abraham did. And this promise is from God himself, who makes the dead live again and speaks of future events with as much certainty as though they were already past.
—Romans 4:17, tlb

You accept me as You did Abraham because I trust You when Your Word says I am healed. Even when I don't feel like I am healed, I say I am healed. For You, God, call those things that be not as though they were.

Therefore I tell you, whatever you ask for in prayer, believe that you have received it, and it will be yours.

—Mark 11:24, niv

I have asked for healing, so I believe I have received it, and the healing is now mine.

I pray that you may enjoy good health and that all may go well with you, even as your soul is getting along well.

—3 John 2, niv

I am enjoying good health, and all is going well with me, even as my soul is getting along well.

The Lord will take away all your sickness and will not let you suffer any of the diseases of Egypt you remember so well; he will give them all to your enemies!

—Deuteronomy 7:15, tlb

Thank You, Lord, for taking away all my sickness and for not letting me suffer the sickness of others.

☙

CHAPTER 27

ASKING GOD FOR A MIRACLE

WHEN WAS THE last time you asked God to do something miraculous? I have heard people say they need a miracle in their finances or in their health, but too often they won't ask for one in faith. God is not our personal Santa Claus, but He does know what we need, and He is not turned off when we ask Him to work miracles in our lives.

I do not want us to be so shallow in our thinking that we place God in a box and think some requests are worthy while others are not. Miracles are divine interventions that defy logic and demonstrate God's glory. Luke 1:37 (KJV) reminds us, "For with God nothing shall be impossible." When you pray for miracles, you are inviting heaven to touch earth. Miracles don't depend on your perfection; they flow from God's compassion and power.

I want you to boldly trust the Lord to perform the impossible in your life. As you do, you will see His wonder-working power in a tangible way. Whether it's healing, financial breakthrough, or restored relationships, God specializes in doing what man cannot. Keep your expectations high. The God of miracles is still moving.

> **God is not our personal Santa Claus, but He does know what we need, and He is not turned off when we ask Him to work miracles in our lives.**

And God confirmed the message by giving signs and wonders and various miracles and gifts of the Holy Spirit whenever he chose.
—HEBREWS 2:4, NLT

Lord, I thank You for confirming the gospel message by giving signs, wonders, various miracles, and gifts of the Holy Spirit as You choose. You are still a miracle-worker, and I trust You to meet my need.

The LORD replied, "Listen, I am making a covenant with you in the presence of all your people. I will perform miracles that have never been performed anywhere in all the earth or in any nation. And all the people around you will see the power of the LORD—the awesome power I will display for you."

—EXODUS 34:10, NLT

Jesus, I bless and thank You for making covenant with me and performing miracles that have never been performed anywhere on all the earth or in any nation. In doing this, all the people around me will see the awesome power You will display for me.

There are diversities of gifts, but the same Spirit...to another the working of miracles, to another prophecy, to another discerning of spirits, to another different kinds of tongues, to another the interpretation of tongues.

—1 CORINTHIANS 12:4, 10

Thank You, Jesus, for the gifts of Your Spirit and for still working miracles today. I ask that You do the miraculous in my life so Your power may be revealed and Your name glorified.

God always has shown us that these messages are true by signs and wonders and various miracles and by giving certain special abilities from the Holy Spirit to those who believe; yes, God has assigned such gifts to each of us.

—HEBREWS 2:4, TLB

Lord, I thank You for confirming Your Word with signs, wonders, and miracles. You have proved that Your message is true through the mighty works of the Holy Spirit. Because I believe, I ask You to release and activate the gifts of the Spirit in my life. Let Your power flow through me so that others may see Your glory, believe Your Word, and know You are the living God.

I ask you again, does God give you the Holy Spirit and work miracles among you because you obey the law? Of course not! It is because you believe the message you heard about Christ.

—GALATIANS 3:5, NLT

Father, I bless You for the precious gift of the Holy Spirit and for the miracles You work in and through my life. These miracles flow not by the works of the Law but by faith in the gospel of Jesus Christ. I believe Your Word, and I stand in faith, expecting Your power to move in me and through me.

THANK YOU FOR MY MIRACLE!

Father, I thank You for every miracle You have brought into my life. Every time I drive my car past an accident, that's a miracle! When I watch the news and know they are not talking about my family, that's a miracle. When the ambulance is rushing by and it's not carrying me or one of my loved ones, that's a miracle! Thank You, Lord, for all my miracles!

PRAYER FOR SUPERNATURAL BREAKTHROUGH

King of glory, visit me today and turn my situation around, in the name of Jesus. Instead of regret, I will become great, in the name of Jesus.

To all the blessings that have been buried, come alive and locate me, in the name of Jesus.

O Lord, establish me with Your favor in the name of Christ, my Savior. Release the restoration You have packaged for me today, in the name of Jesus.

Let my problems give up, as darkness gives up before the light, in the name of Jesus.

All the blessings God has marked for me that are currently not in this country, arise and locate me, in the name of Jesus.

O God, arise and attack my lack, in the name of Jesus. Let the power of liberty and dignity manifest in my life, in the name of Jesus.

Let the chapter of sorrow and slavery be closed in my life forever, in the name of Jesus.

Lord God, usher me out of the position of lack by fire, in the name of Jesus.

Every obstacle in my life, give way to miracles, in the name of Jesus. Every frustration in my life will become a bridge to my miracles, in the name of Jesus.

In the name of Jesus, every enemy forming plans of destruction against my life is exposed, disgraced, and rendered powerless.

I revoke every residential permit seeking to keep me in the valley of defeat, in the name of Jesus.

I reject a bitter life and claim a better life, in the name of Jesus.

Every habitation of cruelty fashioned against me, be desolate right now, in the name of Jesus.

My trials shall become a gateway to my promotions, in the name of Jesus.

જી

CHAPTER 28

RECEIVING GOD'S GRACE AND MERCY

I LOVE SPEAKING ABOUT the divine twins: grace and mercy. When we accept Christ, we receive the benefit of both. Grace gives us what we don't deserve. Mercy withholds what we do deserve. Both come from God's loving heart.

Hebrews 4:16 invites you to come boldly to the throne of grace to obtain mercy and find grace to help in time of need. I dare you to thank God for the favor you have received, which was not earned, for His loving kindness is better than life. Friend, He is the God who covers your mistakes. He is the God who lifts your bowed head. He is the God who loves you despite your weaknesses. Grace empowers you to live victoriously, and mercy reminds you that His compassion never fails. You are not disqualified because His grace is sufficient for you.

> Grace, mercy, and peace will be with you from God the Father and from the Lord Jesus Christ, the Son of the Father, in truth and love.
>
> —2 JOHN 3

Father, I thank You that no matter where I am or what I face, Your grace, mercy, and peace are with me through Jesus Christ. Even when the process is hard, Your presence carries me through. What feels difficult becomes possible—and even sweatless— because of Your grace.

> To Titus, a true son in our common faith: grace, mercy, and peace from God the Father and the Lord Jesus Christ our Savior.
>
> —TITUS 1:4

Father, I thank You for pouring out Your grace, mercy, and peace upon my life. I receive them today with gratitude.

God saved you by his grace when you believed. And you can't take credit for this; it is a gift from God. Salvation is not a reward for the good things we have done, so none of us can boast about it.

—EPHESIANS 2:8–9, NLT

Father, thank You for saving me by grace through faith. My salvation is Your gift—not a reward for my works—so I will never boast in myself but only in You.

Let us therefore come boldly to the throne of grace, that we may obtain mercy and find grace to help in time of need.

—HEBREWS 4:16

Lord God, I come boldly to Your throne of grace so that I may obtain mercy and find grace to help in my time of need.

> **Grace empowers you to live victoriously, and mercy reminds you that His compassion never fails.**

Now therefore, I pray you, if I have found favor in Your sight, let me know Your ways so that I may know You [becoming more deeply and intimately acquainted with You, recognizing and understanding Your ways more clearly] and that I may find grace and favor in Your sight. And consider also, that this nation is Your people.

—EXODUS 33:13, AMP

Almighty God, I pray that I have found favor in Your sight. I am humbled to know You more deeply and intimately through Your Word. I pray that I will recognize Your ways and see clearly Your grace and favor over my life. And I pray You also see it in me.

And of His fullness we have all received, and grace for grace.

—JOHN 1:16

Glory to God! Because of Your fullness, I receive double grace.

When he arrived and saw the grace of God [that was bestowed on them], he rejoiced and began to encourage them all with an unwavering heart to stay true and devoted to the Lord.

—Acts 11:23, amp

Almighty God, I pray that no matter where I am, people will see Your grace on me and view me as a person whose heart is devoted to You.

Through whom also we have access by faith into this grace in which we stand, and rejoice in hope of the glory of God.

Romans 5:2

Thank You, Jesus, that by faith I have access to Your grace. I stand firm in that grace and rejoice in the hope of the glory of God!

We're not keeping this quiet, not on your life. Just like the psalmist who wrote, "I believed it, so I said it," we say what we believe. And what we believe is that the One who raised up the Master Jesus will just as certainly raise us up with you, alive. Every detail works to your advantage and to God's glory: more and more grace, more and more people, more and more praise!

—2 Corinthians 4:15, msg

Lord God, I will not be quiet because I believe and know for myself that it is You who raised me up. You worked out every detail of my life to my advantage for Your glory! Thank You for revealing to the world more and more grace and more and more praise!

According to the grace of God which was given to me, as a wise master builder I have laid the foundation, and another builds on it. But let each one take heed how he builds on it.

—1 Corinthians 3:10

Thank You, Jesus, for the grace You have given me. You are the master builder who has laid the sure foundation, and I am honored to build upon the work You began. Grant me wisdom, discernment, and excellence in all I do so that I may build carefully and faithfully on the foundation of Christ. May everything I construct with my life bring glory to You.

Dear brothers and sisters, may the grace of our Lord Jesus Christ be with your spirit. Amen.

—GALATIANS 6:18, NLT

Jesus, I pray that the grace of the Lord Jesus Christ will be with my spirit. Amen.

He who follows righteousness and mercy finds life, righteousness, and honor.

—PROVERBS 21:21

Jesus, I follow Your righteousness and mercy and find life and honor.

God blesses those who are merciful, for they will be shown mercy.

—MATTHEW 5:7, NLT

Thank You for blessing my life. As I show mercy to others, You show mercy to me.

May God's mercy and peace be upon all of you who live by this principle and upon those everywhere who are really God's own.

—GALATIANS 6:16, TLB

Almighty God, I thank You that I belong to You. I live by Your truth, and I receive Your mercy and peace upon my life. My life is Yours.

࿇

CHAPTER 29

EXPERIENCING RESTORATION

URING THIS JOURNEY to become what we believe, we will need to look to God for restoration. Whether from wounds in our childhood, situations in young adulthood, or incidents that happened yesterday, one thing remains true: God is a restorer. Joel 2:25 promises, "I will restore to you the years that the swarming locust has eaten."

When we pray for restoration, we are crying out to God to repair what was lost, stolen, or broken. This could have happened due to time, messed up relationships, missed opportunities, or stolen peace. God will even restore you to good health. You can ask Him to breathe afresh upon every area that seems to have suffered loss in your life.

Maybe you need your joy, peace, satisfaction, purpose, or hope restored. Maybe you need restoration in your marriage, money, or motivation. Restoration doesn't just bring things back to their former state; it makes them better. The God we serve rebuilds ruins and revives dreams. Trust that He sees what you have lost and will restore—with interest.

> So I will restore to you the years that the swarming locust has eaten, the crawling locust, the consuming locust, and the chewing locust; my great army which I sent among you.
> —Joel 2:25

> *Lord God, You will restore to me the years that the swarming locust has eaten, the crawling locust, the consuming locust, and the chewing locust. What was lost will be restored by Your hand.*

> Thus says the Lord: In an acceptable time I have heard You, and in the day of salvation I have helped You; I will preserve You and give You as a covenant to the people, to restore the earth, to cause them to inherit the desolate heritages.
> —Isaiah 49:8

God Almighty, I bless and honor You. In an acceptable time, You have heard me, and in the day of salvation, You have helped me. Thank You for preserving my life and establishing Your covenant with me. Rebuild what has been broken, renew what has been desolate, and cause me to inherit every promise You have ordained for me.

And the LORD restored Job's losses when he prayed for his friends. Indeed the LORD gave Job twice as much as he had before.

—JOB 42:10

Glorious God, You restored Job's losses when he prayed for his friends. Indeed, You gave Job twice as much as he had before, and You are able to bless me abundantly.

Turn us back to You, O LORD, and we will be restored; renew our days as of old.

—LAMENTATIONS 5:21

Father, thank You for turning me back to You. I am restored, and my past is renewed.

Then He put His hands on his eyes again; and the man looked intently [that is, fixed his eyes on definite objects], and he was restored and saw everything distinctly [even what was at a distance].

—MARK 8:25, AMPC

Lord, You are a restorer. You place Your hands on my life, and now I can see. I declare that my peace is restored, my health is restored, my wealth is restored, my joy is restored, and my focus is restored! Yes, You turned it around!

℞

CHAPTER 30

WALKING IN REDEMPTION

THE LORD CHASES those He loves, and He is eager to bring us back into right standing with Him. That is what redemption is all about. When we are redeemed, we are rescued, made right with God, and forever called His own. You see, redemption could only take place through the sacrifice of our Savior Jesus Christ. When we accept Him, we are no longer bound by sin, shame, or separation. We are forgiven and justified immediately. As Ephesians 1:7 declares, "In Him we have redemption through His blood, the forgiveness of sins."

The prayers in this chapter are specifically for God's redemptive power to rule in our lives. Through them we embrace what God wants to do for us and through us. We embrace our new identity and reject any mindset that would make us speak words of destruction. We openly say, "We are redeemed!" We are not who we used to be, nor do we identify with the lies of the enemy that would bind us to our past. No mistake from our past can outweigh or outlive the love of Christ. We have been redeemed, restored, and made worthy of the destiny He set before us.

When you pray, thank God for redeeming your life from destruction and giving you a new identity. Live from that truth, and you will walk in the freedom and fullness of every promise God has spoken over you.

> In Him we have redemption through His blood, the forgiveness of sins, according to the riches of His grace.
> —EPHESIANS 1:7

> *Father, I glorify and honor You. In You I have redemption through Your blood, the forgiveness of sins, according to the riches of Your grace.*

> Being justified freely by His grace through the redemption that is in Christ Jesus.
> —ROMANS 3:24

Lord God, I am justified freely by Your grace through the redemption that is in Christ Jesus.

He has sent redemption to His people; He has commanded His covenant forever: Holy and awesome is His name.

—Psalm 111:9

Lord, I bless You because You sent redemption to Your people, and You have commanded Your covenant forever. Holy and awesome is Your name.

> **No mistake from our past can outweigh or outlive the love of Christ.**

Remember these things, O Jacob. Take it seriously, Israel, that you're my servant. I made you, shaped you: You're my servant. O Israel, I'll never forget you. I've wiped the slate of all your wrongdoings. There's nothing left of your sins. Come back to me, come back. I've redeemed you.

—Isaiah 44:22, msg

Almighty God, I am blessed to be Your servant. Thank You for not forgetting about me and for wiping my slate clean, leaving nothing left of my sin. Thank You for redeeming me.

He gave his life to free us from every kind of sin, to cleanse us, and to make us his very own people, totally committed to doing good deeds.

—Titus 2:14, nlt

Lord, You gave Your life to free me from sin, cleanse me, and make me Your own, totally committed to doing good deeds.

O Israel, hope in the Lord; for with the Lord there is unfailing love. His redemption overflows.

—Psalm 130:7, nlt

Lord, I bless and honor You for Your unfailing love, and I thank You that Your redemption overflows. Lord, by the blood of Jesus, I am redeemed. Father, You are holy and just, and I honor You for giving me the gift of redemption. Your Word says that I am the redeemed of the Lord, and I declare that it is so!

&

....

....

....

....

PART V

BECOME BLESSED TO BE A BLESSING

God's promises include provision, prosperity, and peace. This section will help you pray with expectation for God's blessing in every area of your life—not just for yourself but so you can bless others.

CHAPTER 31

BELIEVING GOD FOR PROSPERITY

TRUE PROSPERITY GOES beyond finances; it is a state of well-being in every area: spirit, soul, and body. A prosperous person knows the joy of peace. They aren't constantly fretting about the latest headlines, wringing their hands over what will happen to Social Security, or wondering what technological advancements will claim their job. They know God will provide for them, regardless of what happens in the world.

Third John 2 says, "Beloved, I pray that you may prosper in all things and be in health, just as your soul prospers." Our prayers for prosperity are not surface level. We are not just praying for riches; we are seeking God for provision, purpose, and wisdom to steward His blessings. We want the Lord to be able to trust us with the time, talent, and treasure He gives.

God delights in blessing His children, but our hearts must stay aligned with His will. The prayers in this chapter will guide us in praying to be faithful stewards over all He entrusts to us. We need to ensure we are open vessels who can be trusted to give generously and use our blessings for His glory. As we pray, we believe that God will bring wealth and riches to our "house" (our lives) because our hearts and minds are fixed on Him (Ps. 112:3, 7). This alignment ensures that we are not only blessed but impactful with our blessings. This causes our overflow to bless others. So we pray not just for increase but for wisdom to manage our increase well.

> If they obey and serve Him, they shall spend their days in prosperity, and their years in pleasures.
>
> —Job 36:11, KJV

> *Father, I shall continue to obey and serve You. I pray my days are spent in prosperity and my years in pleasures.*

> The man began to prosper, and continued prospering until he became very prosperous.
>
> —Genesis 26:13

Father, I honor and bless You, and I declare that I prosper, I continue prospering, and I will become very prosperous. Thank You for establishing increase in my life and causing everything I set my hand to do to flourish.

Peace and prosperity to you, your family, and everything you own!
—1 SAMUEL 25:6, NLT

Father God, I thank You for peace and prosperity overflowing in my life—upon me, my family, and everything I own. May Your blessing rest on my family and Your favor protect, provide, and multiply in every area of our lives.

> **A prosperous person knows the joy of peace.**

This Book of the Law shall not depart from your mouth, but you shall read [and meditate on] it day and night, so that you may be careful to do [everything] in accordance with all that is written in it; for then you will make your way prosperous, and then you will be successful.
—JOSHUA 1:8, AMP

God Almighty, Your Word shall not leave my mouth. I meditate on it day and night. I pray that I am careful to do everything that is written in Your Word because as I walk in obedience to Your Word, my way will be made prosperous, and I shall be successful.

For there the seed will produce peace and prosperity; the vine will yield its fruit, and the ground will produce its increase, and the heavens will give their dew. And I will cause the remnant of this people to inherit and possess all these things.
—ZECHARIAH 8:12, AMP

Lord God, I declare the seed I sow will produce peace and prosperity. The vine will yield its fruit, the ground will produce increase, and the heavens will give their dew. As one of Your people, I will inherit and possess all these things. I receive the promises You have prepared, and I walk in the blessings You have ordained for me.

May God prosper you and your family and multiply everything you own.

—1 SAMUEL 25:6, TLB

Lord Jesus, thank You for prospering me and my family and multiplying everything I own.

Now in my prosperity I said, "I shall never be moved."

—PSALM 30:6

Almighty God, my prosperity is now, and I shall never be moved.

Using a dull ax requires great strength, so sharpen the blade. That's the value of wisdom; it helps you succeed.

—ECCLESIASTES 10:10, NLT

Lord God, help me stay sharp and walk in wisdom. This is what is needed for overall success.

He himself shall dwell in prosperity, and his descendants shall inherit the earth.

—PSALM 25:13

Father, You are such an amazing God! I declare that I shall dwell in prosperity, and my descendants shall inherit the earth.

Save now, I pray, O LORD; O LORD, I pray, send now prosperity.

—PSALM 118:25

Lord, save now—and send prosperity now!

Enjoy prosperity whenever you can, and when hard times strike, realize that God gives one as well as the other—so that everyone will realize that nothing is certain in this life.

—ECCLESIASTES 7:14, TLB

Jesus, I pray that I enjoy prosperity when I can, and when the hard times come, help me remember that God gives one as well as the other. Through You I realize nothing is certain in my life.

For I know the thoughts that I think toward you, says the
LORD, thoughts of peace and not of evil, to give you a future
and a hope.

—JEREMIAH 29:11

*Father, I thank You for Your thoughts toward me—thoughts of
peace and not of evil. I am grateful for the future and the hope
You have prepared for me.*

So keep the words of this covenant and obey them, so that you
may prosper and be successful in everything that you do.

—DEUTERONOMY 29:9, AMP

*Yes, Lord, I shall keep covenant with You and obey Your Words
so that I may prosper and be a success in all I do.*

Then the LORD your God will bring you to the land which your
fathers possessed, and you shall possess it. He will prosper you
and multiply you more than your fathers.

—DEUTERONOMY 30:5

*Thank You, Father, for bringing me into the land of promise. I
praise You for prospering me and multiplying me beyond the generations before me. May I steward this blessing with wisdom and
faithfulness and that Your covenant and favor continue through
every generation after me.*

Be strong and very courageous. Be careful to obey all the
instructions Moses gave you. Do not deviate from them,
turning either to the right or to the left. Then you will be successful in everything you do.

—JOSHUA 1:7, NLT

*Almighty God, through You I am strong and very courageous. I
shall be careful to obey the instructions in Your Word. I will not
deviate from them, neither turning to the right nor the left. As I
walk in Your ways, I thank You for making me successful in all
that I do.*

And in every work that he began in the service of the house of God, in the law and in the commandment, to seek his God, he did it with all his heart. So he prospered.

—2 CHRONICLES 31:21

Father, in everything I do in service to Your house and in obedience to Your Word, I seek You with all my heart. Because my heart is set on pleasing You, I thank You that You cause me to prosper in all that I do.

Blessed is the man who walks not in the counsel of the ungodly, nor stands in the path of sinners, nor sits in the seat of the scornful; but his delight is in the law of the LORD, and in His law he meditates day and night. He shall be like a tree, planted by the rivers of water, that brings forth its fruit in its season, whose leaf also shall not wither; and whatever he does shall prosper.

—PSALM 1:1–3

Dear God, thank You for making me like a tree planted by the rivers of water that brings fruit in its season, whose leaves also shall not wither. Because I delight in Your Word and walk in Your ways, whatever I do prospers.

No weapon formed against you shall prosper, and every tongue which rises against you in judgment you shall condemn. This is the heritage of the servants of the LORD, and their righteousness is from Me, says the LORD.

—ISAIAH 54:17

I declare that no weapon formed against me will prosper and every word spoken against me in judgment, the Lord shall condemn. This is the heritage of Your servants, Lord. My righteousness is from You.

For I am sowing peace and prosperity among you. Your crops will prosper; the grapevines will be weighted down with fruit; the ground will be fertile, with plenty of rain; all these blessings will be given to the people left in the land.

—ZECHARIAH 8:12, TLB

Father, I honor and bless You. Thank You for sowing peace and prosperity into my life. Because of Your goodness, the seeds I plant will prosper, and my grapevines will be heavy with fruit. Thank You for fertile ground and much rain. Thank You for all these blessings You release into my life.

Beloved, I pray that you may prosper in all things and be in health, just as your soul prospers.

—3 JOHN 2

Lord Jesus, I thank You that I prosper in every area of my life—spirit, soul, and body. I declare that health, favor, and abundance follow me because Your Word is alive in me. My prosperous lifestyle is contagious and generational. Because of my peace, I'm prosperous. Because of my health, I'm prosperous. Because of my surrender to Your will, I am prosperous! I walk in divine prosperity, and everything connected to me is fruitful and blessed.

෮

CHAPTER 32

FINDING PEACE IN THE MIDST OF CHAOS

T HE THINGS WE need in life are not always tangible. Sometimes we need God to be our peace during a difficult situation. Peace is not the absence of problems—it is the presence of God in the midst of them. When Jesus said, "Peace I leave with you, My peace I give to you...let not your heart be troubled" (John 14:27), He was reminding the disciples that no matter their current situation, He was there to guide them through it. In prayer, we tap into supernatural peace, the kind that calms storms, silences anxiety, and steadies our hearts. When everything around us is uncertain, God's peace becomes our anchor.

Through prayer, we can release every burden, fear, anxious thought, and uncertainty. As we abide in Him, the spirit of peace will grow in us. So invite the Prince of Peace into your day, your mind, and your decisions. Let peace be your posture and your portion.

And the peace of God, which surpasses all understanding, will guard your hearts and minds through Christ Jesus.
—PHILIPPIANS 4:7

Father, I am blessed because I have the peace of God, which surpasses all understanding and will guard my heart and mind through Christ Jesus. No matter what noise or distraction this nation, my family, my finances, or any circumstance tries to surround me with, I will proclaim the peace of God over it all! I decree and declare it is You, God, who keeps me in perfect peace when my mind is stayed on You—not just today but every day!

Now the fruit of righteousness is sown in peace by those who make peace.
—JAMES 3:18

Lord God, help me to sow the fruit of righteousness in peace by making peace.

Now may the God of hope fill you with all joy and peace in believing, that you may abound in hope by the power of the Holy Spirit.

—ROMANS 15:13

Jesus, I pray the God of hope fill me with all joy and peace in believing, that I may abound in hope by the power of the Holy Spirit.

The LORD will fight for you, and you shall hold your peace.

—EXODUS 14:14

Father, I am grateful because You will fight for me, and all I have to do is be quiet!

I will lie down in peace and sleep, for though I am alone, O Lord, you will keep me safe.

—PSALM 4:8, TLB

Lord God, because of You I lie down in peace. I go to sleep knowing I am not alone and that You keep me safe.

God makes his people strong. God gives his people peace.

—PSALM 29:11, MSG

Jesus, thank You for making me strong and giving me peace!

Depart from evil and do good; seek peace and pursue it.

—PSALM 34:14

Almighty God, I pray that I depart from evil and do good. I shall seek peace and pursue it!

The lowly will possess the land and will live in peace and prosperity.

—PSALM 37:11, NLT

Lord, I humbly decree and declare I shall possess the land and live in peace and prosperity!

My son, do not forget my law, but let your heart keep my commands; for length of days and long life and peace they will add to you.

—PROVERBS 3:1–2

Abba Father, I will not forget Your Word, for it will add to me length of days, long life, and peace.

> **Peace is not the absence of problems—it is the presence of God in the midst of them.**

When a man's ways please the LORD, he makes even his enemies to be at peace with him.

—PROVERBS 16:7, AMP

Jesus, I ask that my ways always please You and that my enemies will be at peace with me.

Moreover I will make a covenant of peace with them, and it shall be an everlasting covenant with them; I will establish them and multiply them, and I will set My sanctuary in their midst forevermore.

—EZEKIEL 37:26

Lord, I honor and bless You for Your everlasting promise of peace with me. It is You who establishes and multiplies me. Your sanctuary is forever. Thank You for multiplying the work of my hands and surrounding me with Your favor. You are my peace, my stability, and my increase.

You will keep him in perfect peace, whose mind is stayed on You, because he trusts in You.

—ISAIAH 26:3

Glory be to God. You keep me in perfect peace when I am constantly thinking of You because I trust You.

Lord, grant us peace, for all we have and are has come from you.

—ISAIAH 26:12, TLB

Father, thank You for granting me Your peace. All I have and all I am comes from You. Bless God!

Peace I leave with you, My peace I give to you; not as the world gives, do I give to you. Let not your heart be troubled, neither let it be afraid.

—John 14:27

Father, thank You for the gift of Your peace, given to me by Your Spirit. Because of Your peace, which is unlike what the world gives, my heart is not troubled, nor am I afraid.

If you do this thing, and God so commands you, then you will be able to endure, and all this people will also go to their place in peace.

—Exodus 18:23

Almighty God, I realize if I do as You command, I will be able to endure and go in peace.

Blessed are the peacemakers, for they shall be called sons of God.

—Matthew 5:9

Lord, I decree and declare that I am blessed because I am a peacemaker and a son of God.

He got up, rebuked the wind and said to the waves, "Quiet! Be still!" Then the wind died down and it was completely calm.

—Mark 4:39, niv

Just like Jesus, I shall rebuke the wind and waves. In Jesus' name, when I tell them to be still, I will see them calm completely.

Glory to God in the highest, and on earth peace, goodwill toward men!

—Luke 2:14

I give glory to God in the highest! Because of Jesus, His peace rules in my heart and in the earth. I walk in divine favor and goodwill today. *Strife and confusion have no place in me. The glory of God rests upon my life, and His peace flows through me to others.*

According to the foreknowledge of God the Father by the sanctifying work of the Spirit to be obedient to Jesus Christ and to be sprinkled with His blood: May grace and peace [that special sense of spiritual well-being] be yours in increasing abundance [as you walk closely with God].

—1 Peter 1:2, amp

Father God, may grace and peace be mine in increasing abundance as I walk closely with You.

Turn away from evil and do good. Search for peace, and work to maintain it.

—1 Peter 3:11, nlt

I decree and declare that I shall turn away from evil, do good, find peace, and maintain it.

But the wisdom that comes from heaven is first of all pure and full of quiet gentleness. Then it is peace-loving and courteous. It allows discussion and is willing to yield to others; it is full of mercy and good deeds. It is wholehearted and straightforward and sincere.

—James 3:17, tlb

Lord, I declare that I walk in the wisdom that comes from heaven. My thoughts are pure, my spirit is gentle, and my words bring peace. I am courteous, humble, and willing to yield when needed. I am full of mercy and good deeds, sincere in heart, and steadfast in truth. God's wisdom governs my life today.

And through [the intervention of] the Son to reconcile all things to Himself, making peace [with believers] through the blood of His cross; through Him, [I say,] whether things on earth or things in heaven.

—Colossians 1:20, amp

Almighty God, through the blood of Jesus' cross, all things in my life are reconciled to You. Peace reigns in my heart, my home, and my relationships. What was broken is restored. What was lost is redeemed. I am made whole through Christ, and His peace governs all that concerns me.

Endeavoring to keep the unity of the Spirit in the bond of peace.
—EPHESIANS 4:3

Father, I shall keep the unity of Spirit in the bond of peace.

ॐ

CHAPTER 33

RECEIVING GOD'S BLESSING OVER YOUR LIFE

WHETHER YOU BELIEVE it or not, the Lord wants to bless you. He wants you to have a life that is full of abundance, because you belong to Him. Blessing is not just material—it is the favor, presence, and approval of God. In Numbers 6:24–26, the priestly blessing begins, "The LORD bless you and keep you; the LORD make His face shine upon you."

When we pray for blessings, we are asking for divine enablement, open doors, and protection that only God can give. It's not about luck—it's about covenant. You are already blessed in Christ (Eph. 1:3), and you must begin to speak that blessing over your life, your family, and your endeavors.

The blessings of the Lord make us rich, and He adds no sorrow to it (Prov. 10:22). He blesses our minds, hands, and decisions. Remember this: The more we are blessed, the more we are able to bless others. We are not to hoard our blessings; we are to be an extension of God's hands here on earth. As God blesses you, be a blessing to others.

> The blessing of the LORD makes *one* rich, and He adds no sorrow with it.
>
> —PROVERBS 10:22

> Father, I declare that the blessing from You makes me rich, and You add no sorrow to it.

> I will make you a great nation; I will bless you and make your name great; and you shall be a blessing.
>
> —GENESIS 12:2

> Lord God, I thank You for blessing me and making my name great that I may be a blessing.

Blessed be the God and Father of our Lord Jesus Christ, who
has blessed us with every spiritual blessing in the heavenly
places in Christ.

—Ephesians 1:3

Father God, I bless Your name, and I thank You for blessing me
with every spiritual blessing in the heavenly places in Christ.

"Bring all the tithes into the storehouse so there will be enough
food in my Temple. If you do," says the Lord of Heaven's
Armies, "I will open the windows of heaven for you. I will pour
out a blessing so great you won't have enough room to take it in!
Try it! Put me to the test!"

—Malachi 3:10, nlt

Lord God, because You bless me with so much, I bring all the tithes
into the storehouse so there will be enough food in Your house.
Thank You for opening the windows of heaven for me. You will
pour out a blessing so great I won't have enough room to take it in!

Behold, I set before you today a blessing and a curse: the
blessing, if you obey the commandments of the Lord your
God; which I command you today.

—Deuteronomy 11:26–27

Father, every day You set before me a blessing and a curse. I decree
and declare that the blessings that come when I obey Your com-
mandments are for me today.

And all these blessings shall come upon you and overtake you,
because you obey the voice of the Lord your God.

—Deuteronomy 28:2

Jesus, I thank You for all the blessings that shall come upon me
and overtake me as I obey the voice of the Lord my God.

The Lord will guarantee a blessing on everything you do and
will fill your storehouses with grain. The Lord your God will
bless you in the land he is giving you.

—Deuteronomy 28:8, nlt

Father God, I rejoice, knowing You will guarantee a blessing on everything I do and will fill my storehouses with grain. Thank You for blessing me in the land You have given me.

Therefore now let it please You to bless the house of Your servant, that it may continue forever before You; for You, O Lord God, have spoken it, and with Your blessing let [his] house be blessed forever.

—2 Samuel 7:29, amp

Almighty God, bless my house. May it continue forever in Your will, and may it be blessed forever!

Surely blessing I will bless you, and multiplying I will multiply you.

—Hebrews 6:14

Yes, Lord, I receive Your blessing, for surely You will bless me, and in multiplying, You shall multiply me!

Behold, I have received a command to bless; He has blessed, and I cannot reverse it.

—Numbers 23:20

Father, I bless You, for when You receive a command to bless, it cannot be changed.

৪৩

CHAPTER 34

RESTORING JOY AND GLADNESS

Joy is a spiritual force that cannot be stolen. It is your strength, according to Nehemiah 8:10. Gladness flows from knowing God is for you, with you, and in you. When we pray for joy, we're not asking for fleeting happiness but for enduring strength in trials.

Psalm 30:5 (KJV) says, "Weeping may endure for a night, but joy comes in the morning." We can declare in prayer that we receive the oil of joy and a garment of praise, according to Isaiah 61:3. Even in hard times, joy is a choice and a gift.

Joy shifts the atmosphere and reveals the goodness of God, so go boldly before the Lord and ask Him to fill you with unspeakable joy.

> Now to Him who is able to keep you from stumbling, and to present you faultless before the presence of His glory with exceeding joy.
>
> —JUDE 24

Father, thank You for keeping me from stumbling and presenting me faultless before the presence of Your glory with exceeding joy.

> Those who have been ransomed by the LORD will return. They will enter Jerusalem singing, crowned with everlasting joy. Sorrow and mourning will disappear, and they will be filled with joy and gladness.
>
> —ISAIAH 35:10, NLT

Lord God, You have ransomed me, and I will come before You singing and crowned with everlasting joy. In the name of Jesus, I declare that sorrow and mourning will disappear, and I will be filled with joy and gladness.

> Also in the day of your gladness, in your appointed feasts, and at the beginning of your months, you shall blow the trumpets

over your burnt offerings and over the sacrifices of your peace offerings; and they shall be a memorial for you before your God: I am the LORD your God.

—NUMBERS 10:10

Lord God, I honor and bless You. In the day of gladness, I lift my praise like a trumpet before You. Let my worship and thanksgiving be a memorial before You, for You are the Lord my God.

But let all who take refuge in you rejoice; let them sing joyful praises forever. Spread your protection over them, that all who love your name may be filled with joy.

—PSALM 5:11, NLT

Lord, I take refuge in You and rejoice. I sing joyful praises forever. Spread Your protection over me so that all who love Your name may be filled with joy.

> **When we pray for joy, we're not asking for fleeting happiness but for enduring strength in trials.**

Now may the God of hope fill you with all joy and peace in believing, that you may abound in hope by the power of the Holy Spirit.

—ROMANS 15:13

God of hope, I thank You for filling me with all joy and peace that I may abound in hope by the power of the Holy Spirit.

You will give me back my life and give me wonderful joy in your presence.

—ACTS 2:28, TLB

Lord, I thank You for giving me back my life and wonderful joy in Your presence!

But my life is worth nothing to me unless I use it for finishing the work assigned me by the Lord Jesus—the work of telling others the Good News about the wonderful grace of God.

—ACTS 20:24, NLT

Lord, like Paul, I say that my life is worth nothing to me unless I use it to finish the work You have assigned me. And that work is to boldly proclaim the gospel and share the wonderful grace of God wherever I go. I will not quit, retreat, or be distracted. I live to fulfill my divine assignment and bring glory to Your name.

But that does not mean we want to dominate you by telling you how to put your faith into practice. We want to work together with you so you will be full of joy, for it is by your own faith that you stand firm.

—2 Corinthians 1:24, nlt

Sovereign Father, I appreciate You not dominating but teaching me how to put my faith into practice. Working together with You allows me to be full of joy, full of faith, and able to stand firm. Let my joy be unshakable and my confidence in You firm, knowing that it is by faith I stand secure.

Fulfill my joy by being like-minded, having the same love, being of one accord, of one mind.

—Philippians 2:2

I decree and declare that I am full of joy and divinely connected with others who are like-minded, being of one accord and of one mind.

When I pray for you, my heart is full of joy.

—Philippians 1:4, tlb

Father, I am blessed when I pray for others. It fills my heart with joy.

We also pray that you will be strengthened with all his glorious power so you will have all the endurance and patience you need. May you be filled with joy.

—Colossians 1:11, nlt

Lord God, strengthen me with Your glorious power so that I can endure and stay patient. Lord, let me be full of joy!

You paid careful attention to the way we lived among you, and determined to live that way yourselves. In imitating us, you imitated the Master. Although great trouble accompanied the Word, you were able to take great joy from the Holy Spirit!— taking the trouble with the joy, the joy with the trouble.

—1 Thessalonians 1:6, msg

Almighty God, I pray that as others watch me and how I live, they see You in me because it is You who I imitate. Although I may have great trouble, I have great joy from the Holy Spirit. So I take on the trouble with nothing but joy!

You have turned my mourning into dancing for me; You have taken off my sackcloth and clothed me with joy.

—Psalm 30:11, amp

I thank You, Lord, for there is no more mourning in me; instead, I dance because You have changed my garments and clothed me with joy!

Honor and majesty are before Him; strength and gladness are in His place.

—1 Chronicles 16:27

God, I bless and honor You. You are majestic and give me strength and gladness.

That I may see the benefit of Your chosen ones, that I may rejoice in the gladness of Your nation, that I may glory with Your inheritance.

—Psalm 106:5

Father, I thank You for benefiting me as Your chosen one. I rejoice and am glad and see Your glory in Your inheritance.

You have loved righteousness [You have delighted in integrity, virtue, and uprightness in purpose, thought, and action] and You have hated lawlessness (injustice and iniquity). Therefore God, [even] Your God (Godhead), has anointed You with the oil of exultant joy and gladness above and beyond Your companions.

—Hebrews 1:9, ampc

Lord, make me more like Jesus. Teach me to love righteousness and to delight in integrity, purity, and uprightness in all my thoughts and actions. Give me a heart that hates injustice and refuses compromise. As I walk in obedience and truth, anoint me with the oil of joy and gladness. Let Your Spirit overflow in me, setting me apart to reflect Your character and glory.

৪৩

CHAPTER 35

EXPERIENCING SUCCESS IN WHAT YOU DO

Success in God's eyes is obedience, not just achievement. Joshua 1:8 says that meditating on God's Word leads to good success. When we pray for success, we are praying for clarity, favor, endurance, and fruitfulness in our God-given assignments.

True success includes peace, integrity, and legacy. As we pray for success, we are asking the Lord to make us prosperous in all we do as we remain aligned in Him. We are seeking wisdom, diligence, and His perfect timing. We do not accept the world's definition of success because we are not to build our lives on pride and comparison. Instead, we set our minds on kingdom success because we know it is sustained through Christ, is purposeful, and is multiplied to bless others.

> Solomon completed building The Temple of God and the royal palace—the projects he had set his heart on doing. Everything was done—success! Satisfaction!
> —2 Chronicles 7:11, msg

Lord Jesus, I am reminded that Solomon finished building the temple of God and the royal palace—projects he had set his heart on doing. Everything was done with success and satisfaction! I pray this word over my life!

> Study this Book of Instruction continually. Meditate on it day and night so you will be sure to obey everything written in it. Only then will you prosper and succeed in all you do.
> —Joshua 1:8, nlt

Lord, I meditate on Your Book of Instruction day and night so that I will be sure to obey everything written in it. Only then will I prosper and succeed in all I do.

Their purpose is to teach people to live disciplined and successful lives, to help them do what is right, just, and fair.

—PROVERBS 1:3, NLT

Father, help me in my purpose to teach people to live disciplined and successful lives. Lord God, help me do what is right, just, and fair.

For you will be successful if you carefully obey the decrees and regulations that the LORD gave to Israel through Moses. Be strong and courageous; do not be afraid or lose heart!

—1 CHRONICLES 22:13, NLT

I decree and declare that I will be successful because I carefully obey the decrees and regulations from the Lord. I shall be strong and courageous and will not be afraid or lose heart.

**Success in God's eyes is obedience,
not just achievement.**

The thief does not come except to steal, and to kill, and to destroy. I have come that they may have life, and that they may have it more abundantly.

—JOHN 10:10

Although the enemy comes to steal, kill, and destroy, I thank You that You came so I may have life and have it more abundantly.

As for you, be fruitful and multiply; populate the earth abundantly and multiply in it.

—GENESIS 9:7, AMP

Father, let me experience Your definition of success, which is to be fruitful, multiply, populate the earth abundantly, and multiply in it.

But despite all this, overwhelming victory is ours through Christ who loved us enough to die for us.

—ROMANS 8:37, TLB

Lord, thank You for the overwhelming victory through Your love for me.

Wealth and riches will be in his house, and his righteousness endures forever.

—PSALM 112:3

Thank You, God! Wealth and riches will be in my house, and Your righteousness will endure forever.

And Nehemiah continued, "Go and celebrate with a feast of rich foods and sweet drinks, and share gifts of food with people who have nothing prepared. This is a sacred day before our Lord. Don't be dejected and sad, for the joy of the LORD is your strength!"

—NEHEMIAH 8:10, NLT

Father, thank You for the moments when I can celebrate life. Thank You for helping me smile and know my joy is in You, Lord, which gives me strength.

So the LORD blessed Job in the second half of his life even more than in the beginning. For now he had 14,000 sheep, 6,000 camels, 1,000 teams of oxen, and 1,000 female donkeys. He also gave Job seven more sons and three more daughters. He named his first daughter Jemimah, the second Keziah, and the third Keren-Happuch. In all the land no women were as lovely as the daughters of Job. And their father put them into his will along with their brothers. Job lived 140 years after that, living to see four generations of his children and grandchildren.

—JOB 42:12–16, NLT

Glory to God, my success is through You, Lord. You blessed Job in the second part of his life, and You shall bless me with more than I had before. My children will be blessed, and I will live a long life, seeing generations of my children and grandchildren.

And you shall do what is right and good in the sight of the LORD, that it may be well with you, and that you may go in

and possess the good land of which the LORD swore to your
fathers.

—DEUTERONOMY 6:18

*Almighty God, I shall do what is right in Your sight so that it may
be well with me. I shall go in and possess the good of the land.*

PRAYER FOR BREAKTHROUGH, SUCCESS, PROMOTION, AND GOOD NEWS

As you declare this prayer, imagine yourself opening a door.

*As I open my door, I command the door of my marriage to be
opened unto me, in Jesus' name.*

*As I open my door, let every bad spirit associated with me
depart from me, in Jesus' name, and let success and promotion be
attached to my life.*

*As I open the door of my workplace, the power of God shall
destroy every enemy of progress, in Jesus' name. Let there be a
divine visitation in my workplace, in Jesus' name.*

*As I open my door, I declare that I shall enjoy the favor of God
and men all the days of my life, in Jesus' name. My God shall
supply all my needs according to His glory in Christ Jesus.*

*As I open my door, I shake out all evil inheritance and curses
troubling my life, in Jesus' name. Let everything that represents
sorrow, setback, stagnation, and shame come out of my life, in
Jesus' name.*

*As I open my door, let the wind of divine power blow into my
house, in the name of Jesus. I command all my imprisoned benefits to burst open, in Jesus' name. I declare my total release from
demonic captivity, in Jesus' name.*

*As I open my door, let there be a new beginning in my life, in
Jesus' name. I command the evil ropes placed on my life to loose,
in Jesus' name.*

*As I open my door, let the spirit of peace and a sound mind
locate me, in Jesus' name.*

*As I open my door, I come against every evil monitoring spirit
assigned to visit me, in Jesus' name.*

*As I open my door, I open the door of my victory, good news,
and fruit of the womb, in Jesus' name.*

As I open my door, I declare the beginning of growth, increase, and breakthrough in my life, in Jesus' name.

As I open my door, I chase out every demonic spirit hindering my testimony, in Jesus' name.

જી

....

....

....

....

CHAPTER 36

GROWING STRONG IN THE LORD

O NE OF THE recurring challenges confronting the body of Christ is being stretched beyond one's current capacity in God. I remember how my body would hurt as a young boy because I was growing. It seemed like a complete oxymoron that my growth caused pain. But when it was all over, I had become what I wanted to be—taller.

We must position our hearts and minds to accept the fact that growth is not an option. The more we pray, the more we build our spiritual muscle to become what God wants us to be. Spiritual growth is not meant to torment us. It is the process of becoming more like Christ in our character, conduct, and calling.

Second Peter 3:18 reminds us, "Grow in the grace and knowledge of our Lord and Savior Jesus Christ." When you pray to grow spiritually, you are inviting God to stretch your faith, deepen your roots in His Word, and prune what is not fruitful.

If you have ever pruned a plant or a bush, you know you have to cut away the dead leaves and branches to give the plant the capacity to grow healthier, fuller, and taller. So it is with the believer. The Word of God cuts away anything that can cause our spiritual life to dry-rot. From secret sin and pride to fear and doubt, cutting away what is not healthy creates the capacity in us to produce fruit fit for the Father's use. Growth can be uncomfortable, but it is always worth it.

> **Spiritual growth is the process of becoming more like Christ in our character, conduct, and calling.**

Let's position ourselves to grow in wisdom, patience, and purpose. Though painful at times, we will not rush the process because it is how we are perfected and prepared for what is next. Let's not draw back but instead be grateful for even small signs of growth as we trust God's timing in our lives.

From whom the whole body, joined and knit together by what every joint supplies, according to the effective working by which every part does its share, causes growth of the body for the edifying of itself in love.

—EPHESIANS 4:16

Father, I thank You that I am knit together with the body of Christ. Empower me to do my part, supply my share, and help cause the body to grow and be built up in love.

But also for this very reason, giving all diligence, add to your faith virtue, to virtue knowledge.

—2 PETER 1:5

Lord God, for this very reason, giving all diligence, I add to my faith virtue and to virtue knowledge. I will not remain stagnant, but I will increase in every area of my spiritual life. I declare that by Your Spirit, I am progressing, excelling, and abounding in the things of God. I refuse complacency. I press forward, and I will walk in the fullness of what You have ordained for me.

As newborn babes, desire the pure milk of the word, that you may grow thereby.

—1 PETER 2:2

Father God, I desire the pure milk of the Word so that I may grow thereby. I give up the past for growth. I submit to the future You have for me; I proclaim I am growing in mind, body, and spirit!

ಎ

CHAPTER 37

PURSUING TRUE WEALTH
IN EVERY AREA

I T IS NOT acceptable to be kingdom heirs and simply ask God to make us rich. Wealth in the kingdom is about far more than money. God wants to bring increase in every area of our lives—our finances, physical and mental health, relationships, and spiritual walk—so that we are aligned with His will and empowered to carry out His agenda on earth.

Deuteronomy 8:18 says the Father gives us the power to get wealth, but it's not just for our personal gain. He gives us increase to establish His covenant in the earth. Wealth in the kingdom is not for hoarding; it is for impact, generosity, and legacy.

As we pray, we must believe God will enlarge our capacity to receive and steward abundance in every area of life for His glory. We do not accept a mindset of lack. Instead, we embrace God's abundance, which goes beyond money. It's access, influence, favor, and divine connections.

> **God's abundance goes beyond money. It's access, influence, favor, and divine connections.**

With wealth comes responsibility. If we want to live a wealthy life, we must pray for the grace to manage it well, a heart to give freely, and the integrity to avoid compromise.

> Wealth and riches will be in his house, and his righteousness endures forever.
>
> —PSALM 112:3

Lord Jesus, I decree and declare that wealth and riches will be in my house, and my righteousness endures forever.

Those who love me inherit wealth. I will fill their treasuries.

—PROVERBS 8:21, NLT

Almighty God, because of my love for You, I shall inherit wealth. You will fill my treasuries.

And you shall remember the LORD your God, for it is He who gives you power to get wealth, that He may establish His covenant which He swore to your fathers, as it is this day.

—DEUTERONOMY 8:18

Father God, I will remember the Lord my God, for it is He who gives me the power to get wealth that He may establish His covenant, as He promised in His Word.

As for every man to whom God has given riches and wealth, and given him power to eat of it, to receive his heritage and rejoice in his labor—this is the gift of God.

—ECCLESIASTES 5:19

Lord God, I bless and honor You. You give riches, wealth, power, and the ability for me to receive Your heritage. I rejoice for this is the gift of God.

Then you will see and be radiant, and your heart will tremble [with joy] and rejoice because the abundant wealth of the seas will be brought to you, the wealth of the nations will come to you.

—ISAIAH 60:5, AMP

Yes, Lord, I receive Your Word. I shall see and become radiant and will rejoice because the wealth of the nations is coming to me.

Then he will fill your barns with grain, and your vats will overflow with good wine.

—PROVERBS 3:10, NLT

Father, thank You for filling every place in my life with new overflow.

A PRAYER FOR WEALTH TRANSFER

I thank You, Lord, for the transfer of wealth that is coming to me now! No limits and no boundaries can separate or hinder what You have in store for me. The currency is chasing me!

PRAYER TO OPEN FINANCIAL DOORS

By the fire of the Holy Ghost and the blood of Jesus, purge and clear obstacles away from my finances, in the name of Jesus. O Lord, open by fire every door shut against my prosperity and investments, in Jesus' name.

The divine keys to open my financial breakthrough are released by fire. Any evil personality tying down the works of my hands, catch fire, in Jesus' name.

My financial destiny, where are you? Arise and locate me, in the name of Jesus.

I release financial open doors and happiness in every area of my life, in the name of Jesus. Every evil wind sent to blow away the harvest of my efforts, let it dry up and backfire, in Jesus' name.

All my enemies, hear the word of the Lord: You must surrender in shame, in Jesus' name. Altar of poverty assigned against my prosperity, I set you ablaze, in the name of Jesus.

Father, cause the economy of this nation to favor me in my business, in the name of Jesus. I break and loose myself from every collective curse and setbacks, in the name of Jesus.

Anyone who has taken anything from me with the intention to harm me, be disgraced, in Jesus' name. All doors of goodness that have been closed against me, I command them to open today in Jesus' name. I curse every trace of poverty in my life, in the name of Jesus.

Let all demonic hindrances to the sale of my products be paralyzed, in the name of Jesus.

Fire of God, locate and open every closed door against my finances, in Jesus' name. Every roadblock on my way to achievement, break and scatter in Jesus' name. Any door of breakthrough that I have been knocking on over the years, open by fire in Jesus' name.

Any embargo on my access to success, be lifted in Jesus' name. Amen.

A PRAYER FOR OPEN DOORS IN BUSINESS

Let the spirit of favor be opened upon me everywhere I go concerning my business.

Father, I ask You in the name of Jesus to send ministering spirits to bring prosperity and funds into my business.

Let men and women bless me anywhere I go, in Jesus' name.

I release my business from the clutches of financial hunger, in the name of Jesus. I loose angels in the mighty name of Jesus to go and create favor for my company.

I bind the efforts of any staff members who would seek to use evil weapons against me, including lying, gossip, and slander. Let all financial hindrances be removed in Jesus' name.

I remove my name and those of my customers from the book of financial bankruptcy. Father, let Your angels lift up my business so that it does not strike its foot against a stone, in the name of Jesus.

Every good thing presently eluding my business must flow into it, in the mighty name of Jesus.

I reject every spirit of financial embarrassment, in the mighty name of Jesus.

Father, block every space causing unprofitable leakage to my company, in the mighty name of Jesus.

Let my company become too hot to handle for dupes and demonic encounters.

Let all decisions made on my business be originated by the Holy Ghost, in the name of Jesus.

Let my business prosper and have good success in the name of Jesus.

I bind every spirit of uncertainty and confusion, in the mighty name of Jesus.

Let those who would plan to steal from my business be put to shame and confusion, in the name of Jesus.

Father, make me a blessing to my family, neighbors, and business associates, in the name of Jesus. Lord, help me always choose what You determine is best for my business, in Jesus' name.

৪৩

CHAPTER 38

RECEIVING GOD'S GUIDANCE

HAVE YOU EVER tried to take a trip somewhere without directions? For some this would be unimaginable. Yet sometimes we find ourselves trying to navigate through life without the direction of our Father. If you have lived for even a little while, you know that does not work out well. We need the Holy Spirit guiding us each day.

God promises to direct the paths of those who trust in Him (Prov. 3:5–6). When you seek His guidance in prayer, you are surrendering your plans and desires in exchange for His perfect will. His Word is a lamp to your feet and a light to your path (Ps. 119:105). Prayer positions your heart to hear clearly and obey fully. Whether you're facing a major life decision or a small daily choice, the Holy Spirit is your Counselor. Ask Him for the wisdom, clarity, and confirmation you need to continue this journey.

It is not our will but the Lord's that will accomplish all that needs to be done in our lives. Trust that even when the path is unclear, God sees the full picture. He orders the steps of the righteous. Guidance in prayer means letting Him lead as you follow.

> When the Spirit of truth comes, he will guide you into all truth. He will not speak on his own but will tell you what he has heard. He will tell you about the future.
>
> —JOHN 16:13, NLT

Father God, I thank You for the Spirit of truth, who dwells in me. He guides me into all truth and reveals what is to come. I hear what heaven is saying and move in alignment with Your will. The Holy Spirit leads me with clarity, wisdom, and truth every day.

Yes, You are my rock and my fortress; for Your name's sake You will lead me and guide me.

> —PSALM 31:3, AMP

Lord God, You are my rock and my fortress; for Your name's sake, lead me and guide me.

The LORD will guide you continually, giving you water when you are dry and restoring your strength. You will be like a well-watered garden, like an ever-flowing spring.

—ISAIAH 58:11, NLT

Jesus, I pray that You will guide me continually, giving me water when I am dry and restoring my strength. When You do this, I will be like a well-watered garden—like an ever-flowing spring.

> **It is not our will but the Lord's that will accomplish all that needs to be done in our lives.**

He gives the rejects his hand, and leads them step-by-step.

—PSALM 25:9, MSG

Almighty God, when I look at myself, I know I am different. To the world I am a reject, but thanks be to God, You give me Your hand and lead me step-by-step.

They will not hunger or thirst, neither will mirage [mislead] or scorching wind or sun smite them; for He Who has mercy on them will lead them, and by springs of water will He guide them.

—ISAIAH 49:10, AMPC

Dear Jesus, there are moments in my life when I do not know what to do or where to turn. But I know that because of You, I will not go hungry or thirsty, for You satisfy me with living water. I will not see a mirage to mislead me nor will scorching wind or sun smite me, so that I am overcome by the heat of trials. You who have shown me that mercy will lead me in every season, and by springs of water, You will guide me. I walk in Your peace, provision, and direction every day.

This also comes from the LORD of hosts, who is wonderful in counsel and excellent in guidance.

—ISAIAH 28:29

Lord, I know that You meet my every need! You are wonderful in counsel and excellent in guidance.

Dear brothers and sisters, honor those who are your leaders in the Lord's work. They work hard among you and give you spiritual guidance.

—1 Thessalonians 5:12, nlt

Thank You, God, for the leaders You have raised up in my community, church, and marketplace. Bless them, for they are doing Your work. I am grateful for their hard work and spiritual guidance.

He makes nations great, and destroys them; He enlarges nations, and guides them.

—Job 12:23

God, guide this nation, for it is You who makes nations great. It is You who destroys them, and it is You who enlarges and guides them!

To give light to those who sit in darkness and in the shadow of death, and to guide us to the path of peace.

—Luke 1:79, nlt

Almighty God, thank You for giving light to darkness and guiding me in the path of peace.

❧

CHAPTER 39

REAPING YOUR HARVEST

I T IS THE expectation of every farmer to reap a harvest after what has been planted grows to maturity. For the praying Christian, the harvest is not just about receiving blessings; it is about reaping the results of seeds sown in faith. Galatians 6:9 (KJV) reminds us, "Let us not grow weary in well doing: for in due season we shall reap, if we faint not."

When we pray for a harvest, we're asking God for strength to keep sowing, wisdom to recognize divine timing, and humility to handle abundance. Our tears and prayers water our faith, and it's only a matter of time before we reap in joy.

When we pray for the harvest, we do not limit God. We stand in agreement that our harvest will include lost souls and lost opportunities and will promote increase in our land. We believe this because we know our labor is not in vain.

If you desire to reap the harvest of all the seeds you've been sowing, pray the following Scriptures and ask God to increase your faith to the overflow.

> Storehouses for the harvest of grain, wine, and oil; and stalls for all kinds of livestock, and folds for flocks.
> —2 CHRONICLES 32:28

> *Father, I bless You and declare that my storehouse is full of increase—"grain, wine, and oil [and] stalls for all kinds of livestock, and folds for flocks"—so that I may be a blessing to Your people.*

> And sow fields and plant vineyards, that they may yield a fruitful harvest.
> —PSALM 107:37

> *Lord God, I sow fields and plant vineyards so that they may yield a fruitful harvest.*

You have multiplied the nation and increased its joy; they rejoice before You according to the joy of harvest, as men rejoice when they divide the spoil.

—ISAIAH 9:3

Jehovah Jireh, I thank You for filling my heart with the joy of harvest, as men rejoice when they divide the spoil. You cause me to reap the fruit of my labor and to see the fulfillment of Your promises in my life. As You multiply the work of my hands, You also multiply my joy. I rejoice before You, Lord, for every seed sown in faith will bring forth increase. My harvest is full, my heart is glad, and my praise belongs to You alone.

> **When we pray for a harvest, we're asking God for strength to keep sowing, wisdom to recognize divine timing, and humility to handle abundance.**

While the earth remains, seedtime and harvest, cold and heat, winter and summer, and day and night shall not cease.

—GENESIS 8:22

Creator God, I thank You that as long as the earth remains, seedtime and harvest will not cease. I sow in faith, and I declare that I will reap a harvest in due season.

Second, celebrate the Festival of Harvest, when you bring me the first crops of your harvest. Finally, celebrate the Festival of the Final Harvest at the end of the harvest season, when you have harvested all the crops from your fields.

—EXODUS 23:16, NLT

Almighty God, I praise You for my harvest, which already belongs to You. Every good thing I reap comes from Your hand, and I joyfully give it back to You.

A DECREE FOR MY HARVEST

I decree in the name of Jesus that this is my time of harvest. This is my time of being full and never empty. This is my time of overflow and abundance. I speak harvest over my finances, harvest over the marketplace, harvest over my business, and harvest over everything I put my hands and mind to do for You! In Jesus' name, amen.

ॐ

CHAPTER 40

PURSUING REVIVAL

R EVIVAL IS NOT an event; it is a movement of God that starts in the heart. When you pray for revival, you're asking God to breathe fresh fire into dry places. Psalm 85:6 says, "Will You not revive us again, that Your people may rejoice in You?" Revival brings repentance, restoration, hunger, and power. As we ask God to revive us—our passion, our love, our obedience—revival will reach our families, churches, cities, and nations.

When we ask God to send His revival, we rest in knowing that dry bones will live again, and our hearts will burn with the fire of the Holy Ghost. God is ready to pour out His Spirit, so let's keep seeking Him as we meditate on the following scriptures and pray for revival in our lives, in our homes, in our communities, and around the world.

> Revive me, O LORD, for Your name's sake! For Your righteousness' sake bring my soul out of trouble.
> —PSALM 143:11

O Lord, revive me for Your name's sake! For Your righteousness' sake, bring my soul out of trouble. God, I bless You for reviving my mind, my heart, and my ways! The direction You have given me has revived my steps. Thank You, Father! Hallelujah!

> Turn away my eyes from looking at worthless things, and revive me in Your way.
> —PSALM 119:37

Father God, I ask You to turn away my eyes from looking at worthless things and revive me in Your way.

> And we will never forsake you again. Revive us to trust in you.
> —PSALM 80:18, TLB

My Lord, I will never abandon You. Please revive me to trust You.

Turn my eyes from worthless things, and give me life through your word.

—Psalm 119:37, nlt

Father, help me not look at anything that has no worth. Instead, I pray that You give me life through Your Word.

According to Your steadfast love refresh me and give me life, so that I may keep and obey the testimony of your mouth.

—Psalm 119:88, amp

Thank You, Father, for Your consistent love. Your love refreshes me and gives me life so that I can keep and obey Your Word.

> **Dry bones will live again, and our hearts will burn with the fire of the Holy Ghost.**

Though I am surrounded by troubles, you will bring me safely through them. You will clench your fist against my angry enemies! Your power will save me.

—Psalm 138:7, tlb

Dear Jesus, though I am surrounded by troubles, I know that through Your Word You will bring me safely through them. You will put Your fist up against my enemies, and Your power will save me.

The high and lofty One who inhabits eternity, the Holy One, says this: I live in that high and holy place where those with contrite, humble spirits dwell; and I refresh the humble and give new courage to those with repentant hearts.

—Isaiah 57:15, tlb

Lord God, You are the High and Lofty One who inhabits eternity, whose name is Holy. You dwell in the high and holy place, yet also with the contrite and humble. Thank You for refreshing me and giving me a repentant heart and new courage.

God, teach me lessons for living so I can stay the course. Give me insight so I can do what you tell me—my whole life one long, obedient response. Guide me down the road of your

commandments; I love traveling this freeway! Give me an appe-
tite for your words of wisdom, and not for piling up loot. Divert
my eyes from toys and trinkets, invigorate me on the pilgrim
way. Affirm your promises to me—promises made to all who
fear you. Deflect the harsh words of my critics—but what you
say is always so good. See how hungry I am for your counsel;
preserve my life through your righteous ways!

—PSALM 119:40, MSG

*Jesus, let revival in my home, my church, my city, and my nation
begin with me. Thank You for teaching me how to live so that I
may stay the course. Give me insight so that I can walk in obedience to Your Word my whole life long. Guide me down the road
of Your commandments, for I love walking in Your ways. Fill me
with wisdom and understanding so that I am not drawn to the
distractions of this world. Turn my eyes from worthless things and
encourage me to keep going. I remind myself of Your promises,
and I ignore all harsh words from my critics because Your Word
is nothing but good for me. I am always hungry for Your truth.
Preserve my life, Lord, through Your counsel and righteous ways.*

Plead my cause and redeem me; revive me and give me life
according to Your word.

—PSALM 119:154, AMPC

*Almighty God, I thank You for pleading my cause and redeeming
me. Thank You, Lord, for reviving me and giving me life according
to Your Word.*

PART VI

BECOME A WORLD-CHANGER THROUGH PRAYER

Prayer doesn't stop with us; it extends to our families, our nation, and the world. This section will equip you to intercede with authority and compassion, carrying God's heart for others.

CHAPTER 41

STANDING IN THE GAP FOR YOUR FAMILY

THE BOOK OF Genesis demonstrates that when God established the first family in the Garden of Eden, He created His first institution. Prayers that we target for our family and children place us in partnership with God's heart, which leads to unity and generational blessings on our bloodline. Joshua is our role model with his bold declaration as Israel entered the Promised Land: "As for me and my house, we will serve the LORD" (Josh. 24:15).

When we pray for our family, we build a spiritual hedge of protection around our loved ones. Once we offer our prayers through daily intercession, we will see the breaking of generational curses. We can declare with boldness that salvation is released over our bloodlines. We can declare that God sets His divine order and releases it over our home.

Whether your family is whole or broken, or blended or distant, prayer can heal, restore, and realign. Ask God today to be the center of your family. Call each family member's name in prayer and speak blessings over them. Believe that God will bring reconciliation, provision, and protection. As you intercede, know that your prayers carry power and legacy.

So God created man in His own image; in the image of God
He created him; male and female He created them.
—GENESIS 1:27

Father, I thank You for the creation of family. I bless You for creating me in Your image. You created us male and female, and I declare that Your design for family will stand. It is good and holy. I pray that my life and my family will always reflect Your image on the earth.

And God blessed them and said to them, Be fruitful, multiply, and fill the earth, and subdue it [using all its vast resources in

the service of God and man]; and have dominion over the fish
of the sea, the birds of the air, and over every living creature
that moves upon the earth.

—GENESIS 1:28, AMPC

*Lord God, I thank You for blessing my family. I declare that we
shall be fruitful and multiply, filling the earth and subduing it
and all its resources. I pray that we use every resource You have
given us for Your glory and service. May we walk in dominion,
authority, and purpose, ruling over all that You have placed under
our care.*

> **We can declare with boldness that
> salvation is released over our bloodlines.**

Then the rib which the LORD God had taken from man He
made into a woman, and He brought her to the man. And
Adam said: "This is now bone of my bones and flesh of my
flesh; she shall be called Woman, because she was taken out of
Man. Therefore a man shall leave his father and mother and be
joined to his wife, and they shall become one flesh."

—GENESIS 2:22–24

*Father, thank You for the covenant of marriage You established in
the garden. You took the rib from Adam, made it into a woman,
and brought her to the man. Thank You for showing us that marriage is Your design. I pray that husbands and wives will be joined
together as one flesh, walking in unity, love, and strength.*

The man should give his wife all that is her right as a married
woman, and the wife should do the same for her husband: for
a girl who marries no longer has full right to her own body,
for her husband then has his rights to it, too; and in the same
way the husband no longer has full right to his own body, for it
belongs also to his wife. So do not refuse these rights to each
other. The only exception to this rule would be the agreement
of both husband and wife to refrain from the rights of marriage
for a limited time, so that they can give themselves more completely to prayer. Afterwards, they should come together again

so that Satan won't be able to tempt them because of their lack of self-control.

—1 Corinthians 7:1–5, tlb

Lord Jesus, I thank You for the sanctity of marriage. I pray that husbands and wives honor one another, giving themselves to each other in love. Let them not withhold themselves except by mutual agreement for prayer and then come together again so that the enemy cannot tempt them. Father, I pray for purity, self-control, and unity in every marriage so that Your name is glorified.

Wives, likewise be submissive to your own husbands, that even if some do not obey the word, they, without a word, may be won by the conduct of their wives, when they observe your chaste conduct accompanied by fear. Do not let your adornment be merely outward—arranging the hair, wearing gold, or putting on fine apparel—rather let it be the hidden person of the heart, with the incorruptible beauty of a gentle and quiet spirit, which is very precious in the sight of God.

—1 Peter 3:1–4

Almighty God, Your Word says that the greatest honor a wife can give her husband is submission. That, even if the husband does not obey Your Word, they will be changed by watching the conduct of their wife. I pray that wives' conduct will be pure and devoted to You and that they realize it is not their outward appearance—the hair, jewelry, or clothes—that matters to You, but it is the hidden part of her, the beauty of a gentle, quiet spirit, that is very precious in Your sight.

And to be sensible and clean minded, spending their time in their own homes, being kind and obedient to their husbands so that the Christian faith can't be spoken against by those who know them.

—Titus 2:5, tlb

Father, I pray for wives, that they will be sensible, clean-minded, devoted to their own homes, and kind and obedient to their husbands. Father, I thank You that this example of Christian faith will be so remarkable that no one who knows this family will be

able to speak critically about them. Lord, let this family be a living
testimony of Your grace and power.

The heart of her husband safely trusts her; so he will have no
lack of gain. She does him good and not evil all the days of
her life.

—PROVERBS 31:11–12

Lord, for every marriage, I pray that the husband's heart trusts his
wife. I pray that he will have no lack of gain because she does him
good and not evil all the days of her life.

Blessed [happy and sheltered by God's favor] is everyone who
fears the LORD [and worships Him with obedience], who walks
in His ways and lives according to His commandments. For
you shall eat the fruit of [the labor of] your hands, you will be
happy and blessed and it will be well with you. Your wife shall
be like a fruitful vine within the innermost part of your house;
your children will be like olive plants around your table.

—PSALM 128:1–3, AMP

Father, I pray that my family is blessed, happy, and sheltered by
Your favor. I pray that my family continues to fear the Lord, wor-
ship You, and remain obedient to You. I decree that my family
shall walk in Your ways and live according to Your command-
ments. I celebrate the fact that when we are obedient to Your
Word and ways, we shall be happy and blessed. It is done, in
Jesus' name.

Wives, submit to your own husbands, as to the Lord. For
the husband is head of the wife, as also Christ is head of the
church; and He is the Savior of the body. Therefore, just as
the church is subject to Christ, so let the wives be to their own
husbands in everything.

Husbands, love your wives, just as Christ also loved the
church and gave Himself for her, that He might sanctify and
cleanse her with the washing of water by the word, that He
might present her to Himself a glorious church, not having spot
or wrinkle or any such thing, but that she should be holy and

without blemish. So husbands ought to love their own wives as their own bodies; he who loves his wife loves himself.

—Ephesians 5:22–28

Lord God, I thank You for divine order in the family. May couples function the way You ordained. I pray that wives will submit to their husbands as to You and that husbands will act as the head of the wife, as Christ is the head of the church and the Savior of the body of Christ. And I pray that just as the church is subject to Christ, wives will be subject to their own husbands in everything and husbands will love their wives, as Christ loved the church and gave Himself for her. May families reflect the love between Christ and His church.

Fathers, do not provoke your children to anger by the way you treat them. Rather, bring them up with the discipline and instruction that comes from the Lord.

—Ephesians 6:4, nlt

Jesus, I pray that You continue to bless fathers and that they do not provoke their children to anger with harsh treatment. Lord, please guide all fathers to raise their children with the loving discipline and instruction that come from You.

When she speaks, her words are wise, and kindness is the rule for everything she says. She watches carefully all that goes on throughout her household and is never lazy.

—Proverbs 31:26–27, tlb

Lord, I pray that You guide every mother so that when she speaks, her words are wise and kindness rules everything she says. I pray that she watches carefully over all in her home and is never lazy.

Through skillful and godly Wisdom is a house (a life, a home, a family) built, and by understanding it is established [on a sound and good foundation].

—Proverbs 24:3, ampc

Lord Jesus, I pray that every family is skillful. I pray that they will operate in godly wisdom for life. I pray that each home and family

*will be built with understanding and established on a sound and
solid foundation.*

Love is very patient and kind, never jealous or envious, never
boastful or proud, never haughty or selfish or rude. Love does not
demand its own way. It is not irritable or touchy. It does not hold
grudges and will hardly even notice when others do it wrong. It
is never glad about injustice, but rejoices whenever truth wins out.
—1 CORINTHIANS 13:4–6, TLB

*Almighty God, I pray that every marriage is consumed with Your
definition of love. I pray that husbands and wives act with patience
and kindness. I pray that they never display jealousy, envy, boast-
fulness, or pride toward each other. I pray that they aren't arro-
gant, selfish, or rude either. Father, I bless You for teaching us
that love doesn't demand its own way, doesn't hold grudges, and
doesn't keep a record of wrongs. I thank You, Father, for teaching
us that love always rejoices when truth wins!*

൯

CHAPTER 42

PRAYING FOR YOUR CHILDREN

GROWING UP, I used to sing a song in church that said, "Somebody prayed for me, had me on their mind, took the time to pray for me. I'm so glad they prayed; I'm so glad they prayed; I'm so glad they prayed for me."[1] I don't know where I would be or what I would have accomplished if my mother had not been praying for me. Her prayers ensured I would become all God intended for me to become. Sure, like all kids, I strayed and disobeyed, but Mom's prayers reminded me that what God purposed and called, He would perfect.

Psalm 127:3 says that children are a heritage from the Lord. When we pray for our community's youth and children, whether in our family or not, we are praying for our future. We are placing a spiritual covering over our children to ensure that their identity is not found in anything or anyone but Christ. How is this beneficial? When we pray the Word of God over their lives, it calls forth their destiny and shields them from harm. In a world that breeds confusion and compromise, the prayers of the righteous guide our children in the pathway of the Lord.

Position your heart and mind, saying these prayers over your children. We should all want them to walk in wisdom, purpose, and purity, and to be surrounded by godly friends. We should want to protect their anointing because they are the voice for their generation. It is our declarations in prayer that will remind them that the hand of the Lord is upon them. Though our children may seem to be going astray, our prayers will be a light on their dark path.

> Behold, children are a heritage from the LORD, the fruit of the womb is a reward. Like arrows in the hand of a warrior, so are the children of one's youth. Happy is the man who has his quiver full of them; they shall not be ashamed, but shall speak with their enemies in the gate.
>
> —PSALM 127:3–5

Father, I thank You for my children. They are a heritage from You and a reward. Like arrows in the hand of a warrior are the children of my youth. I am not ashamed of them. I am happy, blessed, and joyful because You have blessed me with children.

Fathers, do not provoke your children to anger by the way you treat them. Rather, bring them up with the discipline and instruction that comes from the Lord.

—EPHESIANS 6:4, NLT

Jesus, help me not to provoke or anger my children by the way I treat them. Help me bring them up with the discipline and instruction that come from You.

Train up a child in the way he should go, and when he is old he will not depart from it.

—PROVERBS 22:6

Lord Jesus, I pray that you help us train up our children in the way they should go, because when they are old, they will not part from it.

You children must always obey your fathers and mothers, for that pleases the Lord.

—COLOSSIANS 3:20, TLB

Almighty God, I pray that children will obey their parents because this is what pleases the Lord. Help me honor my own parents, in Jesus' name.

This promise is to you, to your children, and to those far away— all who have been called by the Lord our God.

—ACTS 2:39, NLT

God, I thank You for Your promises to me, my children, and those who are far away and have been called by You. May Your will for my children and our family be done. It is so, in Jesus' name!

Come, you children, listen to me; I will teach you to fear the LORD [with awe-inspired reverence and worship Him with obedience].

—PSALM 34:11, AMP

Father, I thank You for covering my children. I pray that they always come to You, listen to You, and revere and worship You with obedience.

For when they see their many children and all the blessings I have given them, they will recognize the holiness of the Holy One of Jacob. They will stand in awe of the God of Israel.

—Isaiah 29:23, nlt

Jesus, I thank You that when others see my children, they will see the blessings You have given, recognize Your holiness, and stand in awe of You!

All your children shall be taught by the Lord, and great shall be the peace of your children.

—Isaiah 54:13

I declare that my children—and those You have given me to influence in my family, church, and community—shall be taught by the Lord, and they shall be great and peaceful children.

And I will give them one heart and one purpose: to worship me forever, for their own good and for the good of all their descendants.

—Jeremiah 32:39, nlt

Heavenly Father, I pray that my children and the children You have brought into my life shall have one heart and one purpose: to worship You forever—not just for themselves but for the generations after them.

I write this, dear children, to guide you out of sin. But if anyone does sin, we have a Priest-Friend in the presence of the Father: Jesus Christ, righteous Jesus. When he served as a sacrifice for our sins, he solved the sin problem for good—not only ours, but the whole world's.

—1 John 2:1–2, msg

Dear God, I pray that my children remember that You are their guide out of sin. And if they still do sin, they know they have a Priest-Friend in Your presence: Jesus Christ, who is righteous. I pray that my children remember that Jesus served as a sacrifice for their sins. He already solved the sin problem for good—not just for us but for the entire world!

And now, dear children, remain in fellowship with Christ so that when he returns, you will be full of courage and not shrink back from him in shame.

—1 John 2:28, nlt

Jesus, I decree and declare that my children will remain in fellowship with You. Knowing You are coming back, they will be full of courage and not hide in shame.

My dear children, let's not just talk about love; let's practice real love. This is the only way we'll know we're living truly, living in God's reality. It's also the way to shut down debilitating self-criticism, even when there is something to it. For God is greater than our worried hearts and knows more about us than we do ourselves.

—1 John 3:18–20, msg

Lord, I declare that my children will not just talk about love; they will practice real love! This is how they will show the world that You are real in them and how they will shut the mouth of every enemy. I decree that they will know You are greater than all the worry in their hearts and that You know more about them than they know about themselves.

Dear children, keep away from anything that might take God's place in your hearts. Amen.

—1 John 5:21, tlb

Father, let nothing in this world take the place of You in my children's life. Amen!

How happy I was to meet some of your children and find them living according to the truth, just as the Father commanded.

—2 John 4, nlt

God, I decree and declare that my children are living as Your Word commands them to.

For you know how, as a father [dealing with] his children, we used to exhort each of you personally, stimulating and encouraging and charging you.

—1 Thessalonians 2:11, amp

Almighty God, I pray that parents will encourage, motivate, and charge their children!

Now therefore, listen to me, my children, for blessed are those who keep my ways.

—Proverbs 8:32

Jesus, in a world where there is always noise, I thank You that my children listen to You and are blessed because they are keeping Your ways.

The Fear-of-God builds up confidence, and makes a world safe for your children.

—Proverbs 14:26, msg

Father, I thank God that my children fear You, have confidence in themselves, and are safe!

Children's children are the crown of old men, and the glory of children is their father.

—Proverbs 17:6

Lord, I thank You that grandchildren are the crown of old men and that the glory in their lives comes from their own Father!

∞

CHAPTER 43

PRAYING FOR ISRAEL

GOD'S COVENANT WITH Israel is eternal, and His Word instructs us, "Pray for the peace of Jerusalem" (Ps. 122:6). When we pray for Israel, we align with God's heart and prophetic timeline. We ask for protection, spiritual awakening, peace in the region, and the fulfillment of every biblical promise.

Whether Jew or Gentile, we are all part of God's redemptive plan. Intercede for leaders, for unity among believers, and for the eyes of the nation to be opened to Yeshua (Jesus), the Messiah. Our prayer is that peace, salvation, and revival will sweep through Israel, that God would protect its borders, bless its people, and fulfill His Word.

> All these are the twelve tribes of Israel, and this is what their father spoke to them. And he blessed them; he blessed each one according to his own blessing.
> —GENESIS 49:28

Father, my prayer is that all Israel will be blessed, according to Your Word.

> And the LORD said to Joshua, "This day I will begin to exalt you in the sight of all Israel, that they may know that, as I was with Moses, so I will be with you."
> —JOSHUA 3:7

Lord God, I pray that You will be exalted in the sight of all Israel and that they will know that You are with them.

> So let it be established, that Your name may be magnified forever, saying, "The LORD of hosts, the God of Israel, is Israel's God." And let the house of Your servant David be established before You.
> —1 CHRONICLES 17:24

Father, so let it be established that Your name may be magnified forever, saying, "The Lord of hosts, the God of Israel, is Israel's God." And let the house of Your servant David be established before You.

Him God has exalted to His right hand to be Prince and Savior, to give repentance to Israel and forgiveness of sins.

—Acts 5:31

Abba Father, You have exalted Jesus to Your right hand to be Prince and Savior and to give repentance to Israel and forgiveness of sins. May Israel embrace the salvation, forgiveness, and repentance made available to them through Jesus the Messiah.

> **Our prayer is that peace, salvation, and revival will sweep through Israel, that God would protect its borders, bless its people, and fulfill His Word.**

And I will bless (do good for, benefit) those who bless you, and I will curse [that is, subject to My wrath and judgment] the one who curses (despises, dishonors, has contempt for) you. And in you all the families (nations) of the earth will be blessed.

—Genesis 12:3, amp

Heavenly Father, I declare that Israel shall be blessed and not cursed. By blessing Israel, I participate in blessings, for in these blessings all the families and nations of the world will be blessed.

Oh, that the salvation of Israel would come out of Zion! When the Lord restores His captive people, then Jacob will rejoice, Israel will be glad.

—Psalm 14:7, amp

Lord God, I pray for the salvation of Israel. Thank You for restoring them and for causing them to rejoice and be a people who are glad.

Redeem Israel, O God, out of all their troubles!

—Psalm 25:22

Thank You, Lord, for redeeming Israel out of all their troubles!

"Praise the Lord, each one of you who fears him," I will say.
"Each of you must fear and reverence his name. Let all Israel
sing his praises."

—PSALM 22:23, TLB

*God, I pray that Israel shall praise You. May they reverence Your
name and sing Your praises.*

Blessed be the LORD God of Israel from everlasting to everlasting! Amen and Amen.

—PSALM 41:13

*Father, You are the God of Israel—from everlasting to everlasting—
and I bless You.*

At that time I gave this command to the tribes that would live east
of the Jordan: "Although the LORD your God has given you this
land as your property, all your fighting men must cross the Jordan
ahead of your Israelite relatives, armed and ready to assist them."

—DEUTERONOMY 3:18, NLT

*Father, empower Israel to continue to protect and fight for the land
You have already given them.*

Now listen, Israel, listen carefully to the rules and regulations
that I am teaching you to follow so that you may live and enter
and take possession of the land that GOD, the God-of-Your-
Fathers, is giving to you. Don't add a word to what I command
you, and don't remove a word from it. Keep the commands of
GOD, your God, that I am commanding you.

—DEUTERONOMY 4:1–2, MSG

*Almighty God, I decree and declare that Israel is listening care-
fully to the instructions in Your Word. I pray that they not add or
remove anything from Your Word. I pray that they will keep Your
commands and possess all the land You have given them.*

On that day the LORD magnified and exalted Joshua in the
sight of all Israel; so they feared him [with profound awe and
reverence], just as they had feared Moses all the days of his life.

—JOSHUA 4:14, AMP

Father, I decree and declare that You are magnifying and exalting another Joshua in Israel: Jesus. This Joshua will be feared just like Moses during his time.

The LORD has taken away your judgments, He has cast out your enemy. The King of Israel, the LORD, is in your midst; you shall see disaster no more.

—ZEPHANIAH 3:15

Thank You, Lord, for taking away the judgments of Israel and casting out their enemy. I decree and declare that the Lord is with Israel and that they shall see no more disaster.

Yes, take a good look. Then you'll see how faithfully I've loved you and you'll want even more, saying, "May GOD be even greater, beyond the borders of Israel!"

—MALACHI 1:5, MSG

God, I thank You for faithfully loving Your people. May they see Your faithfulness. Be even greater to Israel—beyond the borders of their land.

Then you shall know that I am in the midst of Israel. I am the LORD your God and there is no other. My people shall never be put to shame.

—JOEL 2:27

Father, I thank You for reminding Israel that You are with them; You are their Lord, and there is no other; and they will never be put to shame.

For they are Israelites, and to them belong God's adoption [as a nation] and the glorious Presence (Shekinah). With them were the special covenants made, to them was the Law given. To them, [the temple] worship was revealed and [God's own] promises announced.

—ROMANS 9:4, AMPC

Almighty God, I pray that Israel will never forget who they are in You. To them belong Your adoption and glorious presence. To

them were given special covenants and the Law, and to them were
worship and Your promises revealed.

The Lord also will roar from Zion, and utter His voice from
Jerusalem; the heavens and earth will shake; but the Lord will
be a shelter for His people, and the strength of the children of
Israel.

—Joel 3:16

I decree and declare that You will shake the heavens and earth
from Zion, but You will be a shelter and strength for Israel.

&

....

....

....

....

DON'T STOP PRAYING

As you reach the end of this prayer journey, may you be reminded of this powerful truth: God hears you the first time you pray. So often we allow ourselves to be discouraged because we don't see immediate results from our prayers. Let me encourage you: God is still working behind the scenes.

> **Just because you don't see the answer right away doesn't mean God isn't working.**

In Daniel 10 the prophet set his heart to seek the Lord. For twenty-one days, he fasted and prayed, yet there was no immediate sign of breakthrough. But when the angel finally appeared, he said, "Do not be afraid, Daniel. Since the first day that you set your mind to gain understanding and to humble yourself before your God, your words were heard" (Dan. 10:12, NIV).

Just because you don't see the answer right away doesn't mean God isn't working. There are spiritual battles in unseen realms, but your prayers are powerful, and heaven will respond. Don't let delay make you doubt. Don't let silence make you settle. Keep praying. Keep believing. Keep standing.

Declare these words today:

> *God heard me the first time I prayed.*
>
> *I will not be moved by what I see; I will walk by faith.*
>
> *My delay is not denial.*
>
> *I am strong in the Lord, and I will not quit.*

Friend, you didn't just finish a book; you activated a lifestyle! Don't quit. God will honor your perseverance. He sees your heart, your sacrifice, and your faith. Stay faithful to the things of God. Keep your posture of prayer and watch as He opens doors you didn't even knock on or even imagine for yourself.

Your prayers are seeds, and the harvest is coming. God is not unjust to forget your labor of love (Heb. 6:10). Stay rooted, stay ready, and stay full of expectation. The same God who heard Daniel hears you, and He's already moving on your behalf. I declare over you today: You will become what you believe.

AUTHOR'S NOTE

I'M HONORED TO let you know that the audiobook edition of *Become What You Believe* is read by none other than my mother, Dr. Pat McKinstry.

This is especially meaningful to me because my mother's prayers have carried me through every season of my life. When I was running from God, she prayed me back. When I was broken, she prayed me whole. And when I didn't see who I could become, she prayed until I became what she believed.

So when you listen to this audiobook, you're not just hearing the words on these pages; you're hearing the voice of a mother who travailed in prayer for her son, a woman who knows firsthand that God answers. I can't think of anyone better to declare these promises over your life than the one who first declared them over mine.

To get a sneak peek of the audiobook and hear my conversation with my mother about the truths in these pages, scan the QR code or visit LutherMcKinstryBooks.com/become/resources.

A PERSONAL INVITATION
FROM THE AUTHOR

GOD LOVES YOU deeply. His Word is filled with promises that reveal His desire to bring healing, hope, and abundant life to every area of your being: body, mind, and spirit. More than anything, He wants a personal relationship with you through His Son, Jesus Christ.

If you've never invited Jesus into your life, you can do so right now. It's not about religion; it's about a relationship with the One who knows you completely and loves you unconditionally. If you're ready to take that step, simply pray this prayer with a sincere heart:

> *Lord Jesus, I want to know You as my Savior and Lord. I confess and believe that You are the Son of God and that You died for my sins. I believe You rose from the dead and are alive today. Please forgive me for my sins. I invite You into my heart and my life. Make me new. Help me walk with You, grow in Your love, and live for You every day. In Jesus' name, amen.*

To hear me personally share about what it means to follow Christ, scan the QR code or visit LutherMcKinstryBooks.com/become/resources. I would be honored to guide you through the life-changing decision to accept Jesus and experience His love for yourself.

If you just prayed that prayer, you've made the most important decision of your life. All of heaven rejoices with you, and so do I! You are now a child of God, and your journey with Him has just begun. Please reach out to my publisher at pray4me@charismamedia.com if you accepted Jesus today or if this book has encouraged or impacted your life in any way. We'd love to celebrate with you and send you free materials to help strengthen your faith. We look forward to hearing from you!

NOTES

INTRODUCTION

1. Stefanie Malan-Müller et al., "Probing the Oral-Brain Connection: Oral Microbiome Patterns in a Large Community Cohort with Anxiety, Depression, and Trauma Symptoms, and Periodontal Outcomes," *Translational Psychiatry* 14, no. 1 (2024): 419, https://doi.org/10.1038/s41398-024-03122-4.
2. Bible Hub, "3027. *yad*," accessed September 9, 2025, https://biblehub.com/hebrew/3027.htm.

CHAPTER 3

1. "What Does It Mean to Abide in Christ?" GotQuestions, accessed October 7, 2025, https://www.gotquestions.org/abide-in-Christ.html.

CHAPTER 42

1. "Somebody Prayed for Me," Hymnary.org, accessed September 24, 2025, https://hymnary.org/text/somebody_prayed_for_me_had_me_on_their_m.

ABOUT THE AUTHOR

BISHOP LUTHER MCKINSTRY III is a passionate preacher, intercessor, and visionary leader with over two decades of ministry experience. He serves as the senior pastor of The Worship Center of Atlanta, a thriving multicultural ministry known for powerful teaching, prophetic insight, and community outreach. Bishop McKinstry is an ordained minister with a strong anointing in prayer, deliverance, and faith activation. He has dedicated his life to equipping believers to walk in spiritual authority and live out their God-given purpose.

His own journey of redemption fuels his ministry. Born to Luther and Dr. Patricia McKinstry, he grew up surrounded by faith yet struggled to find his identity. While his mother was preaching the gospel across the nation, Luther's life took a different path: one marked by drugs, gangs, and organized crime. His choices eventually led to incarceration, where he made a pivotal decision to return to the biblical foundations instilled in him as a child.

Today, Bishop McKinstry is a living testimony of God's ability to redeem and restore. His transparency, powerful preaching, and unwavering belief in the power of prayer continue to inspire transformation worldwide. An international speaker, he has appeared on networks including TBN, TBN Salsa, The Word Network, Impact Network, and TCT. He has cohosted *Let the Healing Begin* on The Word Network and now hosts his own program, *The Word Network Live with Prophet Luther McKinstry III*.

For more information, visit LutherMcKinstryMinistries.org.